PROGRAM EVALUATION AND THE MANAGEMENT OF GOVERNMENT

PROGRAM EVALUATION AND THE MANAGEMENT OF GOVERNMENT

Patterns and Prospects across Eight Nations

Edited by
Ray C. Rist

Transaction Publishers
New Brunswick (U.S.A.) and London (U.K.)

Copyright © 1990 by Transaction Publishers,
New Brunswick, New Jersey 08903

Library of Congress Catalog Number: 89-4440
ISBN: 0-88738-297-5
Printed in the United States of America

Library of Congress Cataloging-in-Publication Data

Program evaluation and the management of government : patterns and
prospects across eight nations / edited by Ray C. Rist.
    p.   cm.
  Bibliography: p.
  ISBN 0-88738-297-5
  1. Administrative agencies — Evaluation. 2. Public administration —

Evaluation. I. Rist, Ray C.
JF1411.P764 1989
351.007′6 — dc20   89-4440
                                          CIP

For the International Institute
of Administrative Sciences, whose
encouragement and support made
this effort possible

Contents

Figures

Tables

I

Introduction

Managing of Evaluations or Managing by Evaluations: Choices and Consequences

Ray C. Rist

The chapters in this volume provide a detailed and up-to-date account of both the organization and uses of evaluation in eight Western, democratic countries. With a focus on the national or federal level of government, the material provided here presents a systematic and comparative view of where these eight countries are in their development, institutionalization, and utilization of evaluations.

It is to be expected, and is indeed the case, that such comparative work will demonstrate considerable variability among the eight. But the intriguing issue is less whether there is variability than what the dimensions are along which those differences occur. Key among those dimensions that have helped focus the analyses to follow are the genesis of evaluation efforts, the fiscal situations in the respective countries, the political constellations that either facilitated or hindered the introduction of evaluation into governmental processes, the constitutional features of the respective countries, the availability of researchers from the social sciences, and whether those within government could see uses for evaluation information. Each of these dimensions, and others, are discussed in the chapters that follow. Derlien, in the overview and synthesis chapter (chap. 9), does an outstanding job in synthesizing what we have learned from looking across all eight countries.[1]

What Do We Mean by "Evaluation"?

In developing the analyses of the individual countries, a critical effort included framing the definitions of key terms. Phrases like "program evaluation," "policy analysis," "policy evaluation," "policy studies," "effectiveness audits," and "policy forecasting" were all used, and often interchangeably. Pivotal to our definitions was to distinguish between *program evaluation*, which focused retrospectively on assessing policies or programs, and *policy analysis*, which was prospective and sought to inform decisions that were yet to be made.

The distinction between retrospective analysis, as the focus for program evaluation, and prospective analysis, as the focus for policy analysis, is the result of efforts at definition that began as early as 1965 by Anthony, followed then by Wildavsky in 1969, Poland in 1974, and Chelimsky as recently as 1985. Chelimsky stresses the consequences of this distinction when she writes

> That policy analysis is prospective while program evaluation is retrospective has importance essentially because this fact influences the kinds of questions each can address. The emphasis of policy analysis is on likely effects (or estimates, or projections); a typical policy analysis question might ask, "What will be the likely effects on hospital use if bed supply is restricted?" The focus of evaluation, on the other hand, is on *actual* effects (that is, on what has been observed, what has already occurred or is existentially occurring); a typical evaluation question might be, "What happened to hospital use after bed supply was restricted?" (1985, 6–7)

A troubling aspect of this distinction, and one that the present papers do not resolve, is that these definitions essentially address two sides of the same coin. Good data on what has already happened can have profound influences on thinking about likely future effects. If history is prologue, then it is to be assumed that policy makers would look to what has occurred (and been learned) in similar circumstances before making the present decision. Likewise, once a decision has been made and the impacts of that decision begin to come into view, the likely effects are now transformed into actual effects. Consequently, what appears at first glance as a clear dichotomy—retrospective and prospective—becomes with closer scrutiny two stages of an interactive process: decisions are made, information is gathered about the effects of those decisions, further decisions are made with data available on the results of previous decisions, etc., etc., etc.

The development of program evaluation, both in terms of its methodologies as well as the kinds of questions that it could address, has resulted in a clear expansion of what now comes under its umbrella. The first, and still perhaps main, assumption about program evaluation was that it was a means of assessing program outcomes or effects through rigorous methodological means (preferably via experimental designs).

But the most recent thinking suggests that program evaluation now can encompass the various stages of life cycles of a program or policy — from conception through execution through impact.

This expanded focus and rationale for program evaluation has been institutionalized, at least for the United States, in two sets of evaluation standards published in 1981 (by the Joint Committee for Standards for Educational Evaluation) and 1982 (by the Evaluation Research Society Standards Committee). These standards, particularly those of the Evaluation Research Society, listed six different approaches or strategies for conducting program evaluation. These six — front-end analysis, evaluability assessment, process evaluation, effectiveness or impact evaluation, program and problem monitoring, and meta-evaluation or evaluation synthesis — represent a broad domain of work that can be conducted within a retrospective framework. The recent definition of program evaluation offered by Chelimsky captures this expanded understanding and acceptance. She writes: "Thus, a reasonably well accepted definition might be that program evaluation is the application of systematic research methods to the assessment of program design, implementation, and effectiveness" (1985, 7).

To What Purposes Can Evaluation Be Applied?

If the definition provided by Chelimsky can be expanded to include the retrospective assessment of policies as well as programs (and this is no small expansion), then the evaluation function can essentially be applied throughout the life cycle of a government initiative (see Thurn et al. 1984 for a discussion by four German authors on this point.) The inclusion of policies as well as programs comes from the fact that many governmental actions and initiatives never become programs in the conventional sense of that term, that is, providing health care, expanding preschool education, building treatment plants for water pollution, providing storage facilities for surplus grains and commodities, etc. Indeed, many key government initiatives include such efforts as rewriting banking regulations, changing the tax laws, changing fishing restrictions, or establishing new air-pollution standards. In each of these instances, there is no delivery of government services, no established program that expands or contracts, and no newly established government bureaucracy. Each of these instances represents an administrative procedure that existing government agencies would carry out. Yet for each of these there are consequences that policy makers would want to know about. Whether the policies were administered correctly or had the intended effects, for example, are but two critical pieces of retrospective information.

Taking a life-cycle approach to government policies or programs means that the evaluator can retrospectively assess at least three distinct phases: policy creation or formulation, policy implementation, and policy outcomes or impacts (Chelimsky 1985, 8). In each of these three phases there is a set of retrospective questions that can be posed. While these questions will necessarily vary, depending upon the intended information needs and audience (program managers are going to ask different questions than will the press, policy makers, or legislators), all of them are retrospective in nature. Again, it is important to note that only because of the expanded understanding and wider definition of what constitutes program or policy evaluation can such an encompassing mandate for evaluation be possible.

Succinctly, retrospective questions of interest to those involved with policy formulation or design will focus on what is known from previous efforts addressing a like or similar problem, what is known of the problem itself, and what kinds of strengths and weaknesses of previous designs have to be accounted for in the present effort. When turning to the actual implementation or execution of the policy or program, the retrospective questions are of the type that focus on such matters as the degree to which the policy or program was implemented as intended, how effective the management of the implementation effort was, and whether the delivery system established for the program worked as anticipated. Finally, when focusing on the endgame of the policy or program, the questions turn to matters of accountability, outcomes, measurable effects, changes in the status of the problem because of the impacts of the program, and whether information developed during the course of the effort was ever used to enhance program management and consequences.

Within the context of this brief discussion, it is also possible to distinguish the most likely use of the six different evaluation types discussed above. The first two, front-end analysis and evaluability assessment, are most applicable to efforts at policy design or formulation. Process evaluations, as implied by their name, analyze the implementation or execution of a program or policy. Effectiveness or impact evaluations are those retrospective efforts at assessing the consequences, outcomes, or measurable results of a policy or program. It is in this context that key accountability criteria can be assessed. (Though it also should be noted that accountability concerns are no less relevant when focusing on matters of implementation. One need not wait for outcome or impact data to learn whether an implementation effort was or was not successful.) Finally, the last two of the six evaluation types stand somewhat to the side of the framework presented here. Program and problem monitoring will be ongoing, serving as an indicator of changing conditions and providing feedback into either the design or the implementation efforts. Meta-evaluation, that is, reanalyzing and assessing the results of previous evaluations, draws on the existing body of knowledge about a policy or program. It is conducted only when there is a sufficient corpus of existing evaluation information and when yet an additional evaluation seems less fruitful (more time consuming, costly, complicated, etc.) than turning back to learn what one can from all the previous assessments in the area.

In different countries, different parts of this spectrum of opportunities are drawn upon. Uniformity of effort is not one of the conclusions to be drawn from these papers. What is clear is that while impact or endgame evaluations are generally present in every country (save for Switzerland), the presence or absence of retrospective data for either of the two other stages is not necessarily predictable from country to country.

Managing of Evaluations

Key to the comparative analysis of the eight country reports (and discussed more fully in the summary chapter by Derlien) are the dimensions of the variability that exists in the way different federal or national governmental systems manage their evaluation functions. There is the classic split between centralization and decentralization of the function, with some countries at either end of the scale and others more closely bunched towards the middle. Yet another pivot is related to whether the evaluation unit reports to the executive or legislative branches of government. The groups reporting to the executive branch appear to be more inclined to conduct management and organizational studies or internal process studies while those reporting to the legislative branch focus on the needs of legislative committees for oversight, budget decision, reauthorization, etc. (see Rist 1989).

The third means by which to differentiate among the countries is to assess the degree of independence that the various evaluation units have to undertake their own, self-initiated work. This degree of independence (and it is always a matter of degree) is important in that it gives a sense of the way in which the units can respond proactively or reactively to needs for information. In those instances where the autonomy to establish the agenda for work is limited, so also is the ability of the unit to carry out that work other than within the framework prescribed by those who have the authority to say what the question will be. The inverse of this situation exists for those units which have a relatively high degree of independence and ability to establish the questions to be studied. One spin-off of such conditions is that, in those units where the areas of work and questions to be addressed are largely set by persons external to the unit, the studies tend to be focused on the information needs of the managers, that is, short-term process studies. The ability to ask basic questions concerning outcomes, impacts, and cost-effectiveness carries some risk of antagonizing those with authority over the programs or policies in question. Protection to do so comes through the organizational independence granted some of the units in our study.

Who has access to the reports produced by the evaluation units is yet another distinction among the eight countries. As with several of the other dimensions discussed here, the countries fall along a continuum. On the one end are those who make all or nearly all reports available to anyone who asks. There are no restrictions on who may receive them — legislators, managers, press, public, critics, students writing papers, etc. As one moves away from this end of the continuum, the options split into two directions — one for the legislative users and one for the administrative users. Along the legislative track, the reports produced at their request may or may not ever become public beyond the particular legislative committee in question. If the reports are made public, the definition of "public" may be as narrow as the administrator of the policy or program, or it may be as wide as the general public and press. For the administrative track, the middle ground is to offer the reports to the press and public after extensive internal discussion, editing, and review by senior managers. The report thus released contains no surprises for the administration, since it is essentially their own report. At the other end of the continuum, the administrative choice is to maintain the report as an in-house document only.

The fifth and final means of distinguishing how the various eight countries manage their evaluation units at the federal level is to assess the degree to which evaluation analysis is or is not integrated with traditional auditing. I think it is a safe generalization to note that in all eight countries some portion of the federal evaluation function is presently associated with offices of auditing — or at least had its beginnings there.

In many places this has been something of a forced marriage. But this is to only be anticipated, given that the logic of auditing and evaluation are not the same. Indeed, at the extreme, the logic of auditing is not derived from the logic of scientific inquiry. Financial or compliance auditing begins from a normative position of asking whether or not particular rules, regulations, procedures, or mandates have been followed. The emphasis is upon procedural correctness and compliance with established standards. Evaluation begins from a different set of assumptions — testing hypotheses, ruling out competing explanations, and attempting to answer the causal question, "Why?"

But where auditing and evaluation can come together is in retrospective assessments. Both focus on present or past practices, procedures, and even organizational systems. It has been the ends to which these assessments have been put that traditionally has further separated the two.

Two factors appear to be bringing about a rapprochement. One is that the users of information are asking not only for financial data but for program implementation and outcome data as well. In times of tight fiscal resources, it is no longer enough to simply ask if the funds are being spent correctly. The parallel question is whether spending the funds is making a noticeable and desirable difference. This is one way the two are being brought together. The second is that, just as evaluation is conceptually moving to undertake and develop methods of normative evaluation, so also is auditing moving into work that at least involves descriptive if not causal assessments. In this way, the "comfort levels" between the two are rising as more and more common ground appears. The degree to which this common ground is being used to develop multimethod studies also distinguishes the eight countries.

Stressing these various dimensions in the management of the evaluation function at the federal level makes clear not only that there are differences in the organizational structures and systems, but that these variations will impact upon what can be expected from evaluation efforts per se.

Simply stated, how one manages what goes into the evaluation effort will establish the parameters for what comes out. Centralized units will be looked to for different kinds of studies than will smaller, decentralized units; studies addressing the immediate information needs of managers will be different from those used by legislative bodies in deliberation over budget, allocations, and authorization; work that is self-initiated will have the opportunity to frame a study differently and go after different data than will work that is specified as to question, methods, and scope of inquiry by someone outside the unit; allowing wide distribution and discussion of an evaluation report creates a different climate for change than restricting a report to a "need to know" availability only; and finally, organizing the evaluation function to parallel, if not integrate, with auditing creates possibilities for approaching questions differently than when they are separate.

The eight country reports indicate that decisions about organizational variation and the management of the evaluation function are being made with more or less understanding of the consequences. While some countries are moving to use evaluation in a deliberate fashion and predicated upon an articulated set of goals, others are not so far along. Several in this latter group have come only recently to try and use evaluation at the federal level. Thus, a full elaboration of the intended uses and organization format is yet to be developed. In the interim, multiple smaller-scale approaches are in place. But for both groups, the most important implication is that there exists the basic assumption that evaluation data and analysis are integral to the management of complex industrial societies. All assume that evaluation has something to offer. What can be made of the offering is the subject of the next section.

Managing by Evaluations

Retrospective information can be gathered at any stage in the life of a policy or program. Indeed, it is this ability to span the life cycle that provides one of the important rationales for the introduction of evaluation data and analysis into the management of the federal sector. To be able to bring analysis to bear at any time in the duration of a policy or program is no small feat, and it portends the opportunity for evaluation to make a clear and discernable impact on decision making.

But to have described the potential is not to have described the reality. Creating the opportunities afforded by program evaluation to policy makers is not identical to having those same policy makers take up the analysis and use it. And thus we come to the matter of the utilization of evaluation. This is a topic that has never been far from the top of the agenda for program-evaluation specialists (see Cook and Shadish 1986). How to get their material read and then used in the decision-making process has been of the utmost importance. In fact, if one takes the debates and discussions over strategies and styles of utilization together with the debates and discussions over appropriate methodologies, the major internal controversies of the evaluation community are covered.

Insofar as the utilization pivot of the debate is concerned, it breaks out into two components: when and how evaluation data and analysis can be used. With respect to when evaluations can be used, I would call the reader's attention back to earlier comments in this introduction. The brief remarks on the purposes to which evaluation data and analysis could be put indicated that it was appropriate to consider three broad time frames: policy and program creation, implementation, and outcomes or impacts (Chelimsky 1985). At each of these stages, retrospective analysis could be brought to bear on the existing information needs and decisions to be made.

At the stage of policy formulation, those responsible will have to address several key questions (Meltsner 1976). First, what exactly are the contours of the issue? Is the problem or condition one that is larger now than before, about the same, or smaller? Is anything known about whether the nature of the condition has changed? Do the same target populations, areas, or institutions experience this condition now as earlier? How well can the condition be defined? How well can the condition be measured?

Second, there are a set of questions regarding what has taken place previously in response to this condition or problem. What projects have been initiated? How long did they last? How successful were they? What level of funding was required? How many staff were required? How receptive were the populations or institutions to these initiatives? Did they request the help or did they resist? Did the previous efforts address the same condition of problem as currently exists, or was it different? If it was different, how so? If it was the same, why are yet additional efforts necessary?

Finally, there are questions about what is known of the impacts of previous efforts that would help one choose among existing options. Considering trade-offs among various levels of effort in comparisons to different levels of cost is but one of the kinds of data input that may be available in framing the decision. There may also be data on the time frames necessary before one sees evidence of impact. While one strategy may have a longer developmental stage than another, the question becomes one of how long a policy maker can wait to see results. (And if the results do take a considerable period of time to appear, how did previous policy makers hold onto the necessary support and resources through the period when there were no results to report?)

If all (or even some) of the questions noted above for this stage of policy formulation could be answered with retrospective data gathered from existing or prior evaluations, policy makers would find themselves on considerably more firm ground as they decide what to do. No country among the eight discussed here indicates that they have in place the institutional mechanism to address all of these questions for each new policy initiative considered at the federal level. Rather, some of the countries have some capability. But in the end the issue is not so much one of present capability as it is whether the different countries recognize that data from retrospective evaluation can be (and are) useful during the policy creation phase.

Implementation of federal policies or programs necessitates different information than that needed for policy formulation. It is during the implementation phase that the transformation of policies into programs occurs, when the allocation of resources are to be brought to bear upon the problem or condition at hand. As Pressman and Wildavsky describe it

> Policies imply theories. Whether stated explicitly or not, policies point to a chain of causation between initial conditions and future consequences. If X, then Y. Policies become programs when, by authoritative action, the initial conditions are created. X now exists. Programs make the theories operational by forging the first link in the causal chain connecting actions to objectives. Given X, we act to obtain Y. Implementation, then, is the ability to forge subsequent links in the causal chain so as to obtain the desired results. (1984, *xxiii*)

The research literature on policy and program implementation indicates that it is a particularly difficult task to accomplish (cf. Hargrove 1985, Pressman and Wildavsky 1984, and Yin 1985). Again quoting from Pressman and Wildavsky:

> Our normal expectation should be that new programs will fail to get off the ground and that, at best, they will take considerable time to get started. The cards in this world are stacked against things happening, as so much effort is required to make them move. The remarkable thing is that new programs work at all. (1984, 109)

It is in this context of struggling to find ways of making programs work that retrospective information from program evaluation can come into play. The information clusters into several areas. First, there is material on the implementation process per se. Questions here would focus on such matters as the cost, the degree to which the program is reaching the target population, the similarity of programs across the various sites, the aspects of the program that are or are not operational, whether the services that were slated to be delivered were in fact the ones delivered, and the like. The second set of questions would address the problem or situation that prompted the policy or program response in the first place. Of concern here would be an ongoing monitoring of the situation — whether the conditions have improved, worsened, remained static; whether the same target population is involved as earlier; whether the condition has spread or contracted; and whether the aims of the program still match the condition. The third set of implementation questions that could be addressed with retrospective data concern the efforts made organizationally to respond. Here data would be relevant to learn how the organizational response to the situation has been conceptualized; what expertise and interest is shown by management and staff; what controls over the allocation of resources are in place; whether the organizational structure reflects organizational goals; what means exist to decide among competing demands; and what kinds of interactive information or feedback loops are in place to assist managers in their ongoing efforts to move the program towards stated objectives. It is information of precisely this type on the implementation process that Robert Behn (1988) states is so critical to managers as they struggle to "grope along" and so move towards organizational goals.

The third stage in the policy life cycle comes when the policy or program is sufficiently mature than one can address questions of accountability, impacts, or outcomes. Here again, the information needs are different from the two previous stages. First, there is the matter of what the program did or did not accomplish: whether objectives were met; whether the implementation strategies were successful in moving the program or policy in the desired direction; how much is known about outcomes; whether the original objectives of the policy held through implementation; what kinds of mid-course corrections were made to keep the program on track; and how confident one can be in the measures being used to determine program influence. The second cluster of information needs relates to changes in the problem or condition. Here questions focus on whether the condition has or has not changed; what portion of the change (presuming some) can be attributed to the policy or program intervention; and whether the problem or condition is yet of a magnitude and nature that further action is necessary. Finally, there are information needs concerning accountability. Here the focus is on management supervision, attention, and procedure: whether the program stayed within budget; whether personnel matters were handled in an appropriate and legal fashion; whether records are complete and available; whether attrition was held to a reasonable level; whether all equipment is accounted for and in working order; and so on.

Stressing the uses of retrospective information at these various stages of a policy or program represents a recent change in thinking (see Cook and Shadish 1986). Traditionally, evaluation has been thought of as taking place after the program is completed or when the policy comes up for periodic review. This present discussion demonstrates that the use of retrospective information is applicable throughout the cycle. Thus the debates over utilization somewhat miss the mark if they only address the last phase — that of accountability or impact assessment. The issue is not whether retrospective data have a contribution to make at all stages, but only how the respective governments can organize their evaluation functions to take full advantage of what this resource has to offer.

The second aspect of the utilization debate addresses exactly this question — how to enhance utilization. If the recognition is there that throughout the phases of a policy or program one has a need for retrospective data (that is, when to use evaluation), then the matter of how to ensure that opportunities for use exist is a logical next step. (Note that the use of the term "opportunities" here is deliberate. Evaluation information is a resource available to decision makers. But using it is not a prerequisite to making a decision.)

The discussion will be rather brief on this point, as it goes beyond the scope of the papers included in this volume. How evaluation information is used and the circumstances of that use in comparative perspective need further study. Yet the present studies do give sufficient information on the organization and logic of the evaluation efforts in the eight countries for one to glimpse the presumed outcomes evaluation research can have on decision making.

Stated differently, by organizing themselves as they have, each country has given an indication of the role that it believes program evaluation can play in its decision-making processes. As a most basic example, the fact that all eight have institutionalized evaluation functions within the federal systems — as opposed to total decentralization to lower levels of government or even establishing the evaluation function within universities or governmental research institutes — says a great deal about the value placed on proximity, control, responsiveness, timeliness, etc. It is fair to assume the individual governments think evaluation research and analysis have some worth, or they would not allocate the time, staff, and financial resources to create such units. And having them, what do they expect to gain?

I think the case is rather compelling that the respective governments expect direct and immediate results from their evaluation units. The assumption is that these units will produce relevant and useful information that will be directly applicable to the decision-making process. These units are organized and funded because they are presumed to generate analysis that will make a difference. The underlying logic is that of a linear relation between creating and supporting evaluation units on the one hand and attributable impacts from their work on the other.

This basic governmental assumption runs contrary to the majority perspective in the evaluation community itself (Chelimsky 1983, and Weiss 1987). While policy makers are putting their resources into evaluation units in the anticipation of clear benefits and results, the evaluation community writes and talks of indirect influences on decision making, of social enlightenment instead of social engineering, and of cumulative persuasiveness coming from years of evaluation findings, rather than from one or a few such studies. The evaluation community sees its craft as somewhat fragile, tenuous, and even peripheral to much of the decision making going on in government. In fact, there are many who still hold to the view of James Coleman, who wrote in 1972:

> There is no body of methods; no comprehensive methodology for the study of the impact of public policy as an aid to future policy.

The end result of these differences between the practitioners' and users' perceptions and views on evaluation is that the evaluation function risks becoming like a dog chasing its own tail. It is going round and round, and getting nowhere. Policy makers are looking to evaluators to provide that which the evaluators are saying they cannot provide. Yet evaluators are encouraging more and more evaluation at all levels of government (see Nioche and Poinsard 1985, on France). This disconnect between the anticipated results desired by the users and those promised by the providers will at some point have to be addressed. We can assume it will come first in those countries where the evaluation function is more developed and more institutionalized in government.

This volume thus appears at an opportune time in the history of evaluation. By being able to document and describe the evaluation function at the federal level across eight Western countries, we have an opportunity to observe different stages of development. Indeed, a key organizing principal of the book is that the eight countries represented here fall into two broad categories — one being the countries who developed evaluation capabilities during the "first wave" of such efforts and the other being the cluster of countries who developed such capabilities later during the "second wave" of development. These reports also allow an examination both of where the federal evaluation function has been institutionally located across countries, and of what that means for the information that is generated and the uses to which it is put. All eight countries are venturing in the same direction, if not down the same path. Observing where they are on their respective journeys is the contribution offered by the authors in this book.

On the Present Volume

All of the papers presented here are original contributions. They have taken as their point of departure a description and assessment of how their respective countries have moved to institutionalize the evaluation function at the federal level. The authors are all participants in an ongoing Working Group on Policy Evaluation sponsored by the International Institute of Administrative Sciences in Brussels, Belgium. This volume is the group's first product. The working group is comprised of members from both government and academia. In the present volume, the chapters about Norway and the United States are written by persons working in their respective federal governments, while the other six come from academia.

A note to readers: While books are meant to convey information in one direction, from author to reader, there is every justification and rationale for trying to build the opportunities for two-way communication. To learn of ongoing work in different countries and to find out, via a book such as this, who is addressing these topics can enhance the overall effort at developing better comparative research and analysis.

Networking in comparative research is both necessary and fruitful. Consequently, the addresses of all contributors are listed at the end of this volume. It is hoped that readers will feel free to write the authors to probe points in more detail, or to provide information on their own work that is germane to what is discussed here. Such an exchange is welcomed and encouraged.

The views expressed here are those of the author and no endorsement by the U.S. General Accounting Office is intended or should be inferred.

Note

1. Readers will note that in the overview and synthesis chapter by Derlien, references are made to the present circumstances in both France and Sweden, countries not represented with chapters in the present volume. The reason is that the chapters on these two countries were never completed, in one instance due to the Swedish author being transferred within the government, and in the second due to the French authors' being given major new responsibilities within their own ministry. However, Derlien and these individuals shared comments, and he had access to other papers on each of the two countries.

References

Anthony, R. N. 1965. *Planning and control systems: A framework for analysis.* Cambridge, Mass.: Harvard University Press.

Arvidsson, G. 1986. "Performance auditing." in *Guidance control, and evaluation in the public sector.* F. X. Kaufmann, G. Majone, V. Ostrom, and W. Wirth, eds. Berlin: de Gruyter.

Barbarie, A. J. 1986. "Evaluating government R & D: Beyond 'Quality of research'." in *Performance and credibility.* J. Wholey, M. Abramson, and C. Bellavita, eds. Lexington, Mass.: Lexington Books.

Behn, R. D. 1988. "Managing by groping along." *Journal of Policy Analysis and Management* 7 (4).

Chelimsky, E. 1983. "Program evaluation and appropriate governmental change." *Annals* no. 466.

Chelimsky, E. 1985. "Old patterns and new directions in program evaluation." *Program evaluation: patterns and directions.* E. Chelimsky, ed. Washington, D.C.: American Society for Public Administration.

Coleman, J. S. 1972. *Policy research in the social sciences.* Morristown, N.J.: General Learning Press.

Cook, T. D., and W. R. Shadish. 1986. "Program evaluation: The worldly science." *Annual Review of Psychology* 37.

Evaluation Research Society Standards Committee. 1982. "Evaluation research society standards for program evaluation." in Standards for Evaluation Practice, *New Directions for Program Evaluation no. 15.* San Francisco, Calif.: Jossey-Bass.

Hargrove, E. 1985. *The missing link: The study of the implementation of social policy.* Washington, D.C.: The Urban Institute Press.

Joint Committee on Standards for Educational Evaluation. 1981. *Standards for evaluation of educational programs, projects, and materials.* New York: McGraw-Hill.

Leeuw, F. L. 1988. "Juvenile delinquency and public policy in the Netherlands: Challenging underlying policy assumptions." Paper presented at the conference on Social Policy Research, organized by the Leyden Institute for Social Policy Research, University of Leyden.

Meltsner, A. J. 1976. *Policy analysts in the bureaucracy.* Berkeley: University of California Press.

Nioche, J. P., and R. Poinsard. 1985. "Public policy evaluation in France." *Journal of Policy Analysis and Management* 5 (1).

Poland, O. 1974. "Program evaluation and administrative theory." *Public Administration Review* 34 (July/August).

Pressman, J. L., and A. Wildavsky. 1984. *Implementation.* 3d ed. Berkeley: University of California Press.

Rist, R. C. 1987. "Social science analysis and congressional uses: The case of the United States General Accounting Office." in *Social science research and government.* M. Bulmer, ed. Cambridge: Cambridge University Press.

_____ ed. 1989. *Policy issues for the 1990s.* New Brunswick, N.J.: Transaction Books.

Thurn, G., P. Wagner, B. Wittrock, and H. Wollmann, eds. 1984. *Development and present state of public policy research: Country studies in comparative perspective.* Berlin: Wissenschaftszentrum.

Weiss, C. H. 1987. "Evaluation for decisions: Is anybody there? Does anybody care?" Plenary presentation, American Evaluation Association Meeting. Boston, Mass.

Wildavsky, A. 1969. "Rescuing policy analysis from PPBS." *Public Administration Review* 29 (March/April).

Yin, R. K. 1985. "Studying the implementation of public programs." in *Studying Implementation.* W. Williams, ed. Chatham, N.J.: Chatham House Publishers.

Ysander, B.-C. 1983. *Public policy evaluation in Sweden.* Working paper no. 106. Stockholm: The Industrial Institute for Economic and Social Research.

II

Countries in the First Wave of Evaluation Development

1

Policy and Program Evaluation in the Government of Canada

R. V. Segsworth

Introduction

In a series of background documents prepared for a 1985 seminar on program evaluation, the government of the Province of Quebec raised the question: "What's new after twenty years?" (Program Evaluation Branch [PEB] 1985). The implication that a serious program evaluation policy and function has existed in the Public Service of Canada for more than two decades is somewhat misleading. It could be argued that program evaluations had been conducted virtually from Confederation. Parliamentary committees, central agencies, line departments, and the cabinet had examined and reviewed policies and programs over the years. Royal commissions and, more recently, "colored" papers and task forces were used frequently to examine and evaluate the effectiveness of various government policies and programs (Doerr 1981). On the other hand, it is equally clear that such efforts were sporadic and of uneven quality. There is, however, evidence that suggests that a serious attempt to establish an internal, comprehensive, ongoing program evaluation capability and process began in the 1960s.

The Development of Evaluation Policy

The reports of the Royal Commission on Government Organization (Glassco Commission) stressed, among other things, the need to justify expenditures. The introduction of planning, programming, and budgeting (PPB) in the late 1960s was perceived to be a step in this direction.

21

The 1966 Treasury Board publication, *Financial Management*, pointed out the need to monitor the progress of programs, to evaluate the effectiveness of operations, and to assess the performance of government activities. The 1969 PPB Guide called for an "information system on each program to supply data for the monitoring of achievement of program goals and to supply data for the reassessment of the program objectives and the appropriateness of the program itself." The evaluation implications and concerns were evident.

Departments were encouraged to establish planning and evaluation units during the late 1960s and early 1970s and to use such units to carry out the kinds of evaluation studies suggested by PPB. The Treasury Board Secretariat set up its Planning Branch in 1969. This agency, amongst other responsibilities, carried out sophisticated evaluations and policy reviews, developed evaluation capacity and support for departments and attempted to show the way in an effort to encourage more and better evaluation activities within departments.

The success of such efforts was marginal. Despite the prime minister's apparent support for such "rationalist" attempts (Adie and Thomas 1982), program evaluation within the public service of Canada was largely unsuccessful. Treasury Board studies in 1974 and 1976 "found that little progress had been made in evaluating programs" (Program Evaluation Branch [PEG] February 1985, 8). "The bulk of staff years nominally assigned to evaluation were routinely utilized in broad planning activities, consultancy roles and specialized ad hoc activities" (Jordan and Sutherland 1979, 588). Dobell and Zussman noted that a "solid decade — almost two — has gone into changing the words and the forms. Yet even the most dedicated do not argue that evaluation efforts have led to decisive results or significant government action" (1981, 406).

Dobell and Zussman argue that three factors held back the success of program evaluation efforts: the lack of agreed theory and purpose, departmental resistance, and the failure of the system to consider the information needs of the user. Michael Prince suggested that "probably the most fundamental factor affecting policy-advisory groups in attempting to organize their program evaluation role is that there is no overall process in the federal government" (1979, 295).

This failure to evaluate was noted with concern by an increasingly influential external agent — the auditor general of Canada. Over a long period of time, his annual reports expressed concern regarding financial management practices within the government of Canada. His 1976, 1977, and 1978 reports specifically pointed to a need to improve the program evaluation function within the public service.

Parliament acted to support the auditor general. The 1977 Auditor

General's Act allowed the auditor general "to call Parliament's attention to cases in which the government had not established satisfactory procedures to measure and report on the effectiveness of its programs" (McNamara 1979, 1544).

This officer of Parliament was quick to respond to his new mandate. By 1978 he reported that "a review of 23 programs in 18 departments has disclosed few successful attempts to evaluate the effectiveness of programs. The scope and quality of effectiveness evaluation will have to be increased significantly before management, the Government and Parliament, each with its respective interests, can be reasonably informed on the achievements of public programs." Earlier, in 1977 he recommended the appointment of a "chief financial officer for the government" (Jordan and Sutherland 1979, 585-86).

The Royal Commission on Financial Management and Accountability (Lambert Commission), appointed in 1976, reported in 1979. It noted concerns similar to those raised by the auditor general. The Lambert Commission put great emphasis on the need to improve program evaluation. It recommended a cyclical review of government programs every five years and a policy which would ensure the capacity within government to conduct such evaluations at reasonable standards of quality.

The government had little choice but to respond to such pressures. The Office of the Comptroller General (OCG) was created in 1978. The first incumbent, Harry Rogers, described his program evaluation responsibilities as being

- to develop and promulgate the Treasury Board's policy and guidelines on program evaluation;
- to be collector and disseminator of information which will aid in the performance of program evaluation;
- to provide advisory services on the application to specific programs of program evaluation;
- to review departmental and agency compliance with the Treasury Board's policy. (Rogers, April 1979)

Treasury Board policy had been outlined in Circular 1977-47, which was issued on 30 September 1977. The general statement of policy was that "departments and agencies of the federal government will periodically review their programs to evaluate their effectiveness in meeting their objectives and the efficiency with which they are being administered". The remaining six pages of the circular provided guidelines on the policy.

The period from 1978 to 1981 was one in which the Program Evaluation Branch (PEB), together with the comptroller general, attempted to give substance to the 1977 policy. A serious effort was undertaken to avoid much of the departmental resistance which had characterized the previous effort. Mr. Rogers adopted what he called a "co-operative approach" (OCG Nov. 1979). This strategy of "the soft sell of program evaluation in an era of expenditure restraint" (Doern and Maslove 1979, 3) involved extensive consultation with senior line department officials as well as outside experts. In addition, the PEB staff prepared, circulated, discussed, and amended background and discussion papers (Office of the Comptroller General [OCG] Oct. 1980). By the fall of 1981, the 1977 policy had taken shape and it was outlined in two important publications: *Guide on the Program Evaluation Function* (PEB 1981a) and *Principles for the Evaluation of Programs by Federal Departments and Agencies* (PEB 1981b).

These two documents are the basis of much of what follows. They provide a definition of program evaluation in the government of Canada. They outline the roles of key actors in the process and they discuss the process which is required. In essence, these two publications describe, in considerable detail, official policy regarding program evaluation.

A Definition of Policy and Program Evaluation

Program evaluation has not been viewed in the same manner in Canada as it has in the United States for two reasons. There is less of a history of evaluation as a significant part of social-science research in Canada than in the United States and as a result, government has taken more of a leadership role than has been the case in the United States. The fact that Canada is a parliamentary system with a fusion rather than a separation of the executive and legislative branches also necessitates a somewhat different approach to program and policy evaluation. It is seen as one of many elements in the management cycle — reviewing and monitoring program performance (see figure 1.1). The basic purpose of program evaluation, therefore, is to provide clients and users with relevant and timely information and analysis to assist them to make better resource allocation and program improvement decisions. In addition, it is believed that good evaluation studies will improve accountability within government. As a result of this approach to program evaluation, less emphasis is placed on truly scientific studies that attempt to provide definitive statements about program outcomes, effects, and impacts, or all three.

At the same time, the policy suggests a fairly comprehensive examination of a number of fundamental subjects in each evaluation study conducted. There are four basic program evaluation issues involved: program rationale, impacts and effects, objectives achievement, and alternatives.

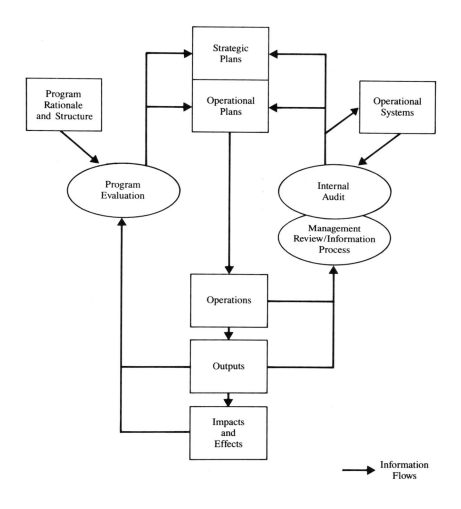

FIGURE 1.1
Management Review and Monitoring Functions

Program rationale raises the question of whether the program makes sense. Two further questions follow from this concern. The first involves an assessment of the extent to which the objectives and mandate of the program continue to be relevant. The second refers to the extent to which outputs and operational activities are logically linked to the attainment of program objectives.

Impacts and effects focuses on results and asks what has happened. In this element, impacts and effects, both intended and unintended, are to be determined. In addition, the evaluator is expected to describe relationships of the program under review with other relevant programs which may affect or duplicate its outputs.

Objectives achievement concerns itself with the question of whether the program has achieved what was desired. In addition, the evaluation study is expected to demonstrate how appropriate results were achieved.

Finally, the evaluator must examine alternatives. Two issues confront him. The first is whether more cost-effective programs might be created to achieve the desired results. The second is an assessment of alternative delivery systems to see if more economical means might be employed to achieve the objectives established for the program.

The Structures of Policy on Program Evaluation

In order for this type of evaluation to be conducted regularly and thoroughly, the policy establishes well-defined responsibilities for a number of key actors in the process. Other factors, including political pressures and needs, require the participation of other actors. Six structures have important roles to play in the evaluation process and in ensuring that program evaluation policy is implemented. They are the OCG, the deputy heads of departments and agencies, evaluation units within departments, Treasury Board, cabinet policy committees, and the auditor general.

The Office of the Comptroller General has a system-wide responsibility for program evaluation. This office, and in particular, the PEB, is to ensure that the 1977 policy on program evaluation is implemented throughout the Public Service of Canada in appropriate departments and agencies. Initially, much of the effort involved the development and dissemination of policy and guidelines. With the publication of the *Guide* (PEB 1981a) and *Principles* (PEB 1981b) in 1981 a major part of this aspect of the PEB's work had been completed. The oversight role remains an important one. This involves assessing the quality of individual evaluations carried out within departments and advising appropriate officials of its findings. It also involves the examination of the operation of the program evaluation function within these departments and ensuring that appropriate corrections and action are taken when necessary. This "control" responsibility is supplemented by a "service" responsibility. The OCG is expected to provide advice and assistance to departments insofar as program evaluation is concerned. In large part, training and consulting activities have constituted the major elements of the service responsibility.

Since program evaluation is part of the management cycle in Canada, it is hardly surprising that deputy heads of departments and agencies have major roles to play. They have overall responsibility for the organization and functioning of program evaluation within their areas of jurisdiction. They are expected to ensure that appropriate studies are carried out and that reports on evaluation findings are submitted to them, and they are expected to follow up on evaluations by taking appropriate decisions. One of the interesting aspects of the policy, which may have been intended to guarantee involvement by the deputy heads and overcome potential departmental resistance, is the decision to make the deputy head the formal client of all evaluations of programs for which he has responsibility.

To assist the deputy head, the policy requires that evaluation units be established in all departments. The *Guide* lists eleven distinct responsibilities which normally would be assumed by such units. In general, it is fair to state that program evaluation units assume responsibility for managing program evaluation within their departments. In addition, they are expected to carry out the vast majority of evaluations required by the deputy head. The policy notes the importance of creating identifiable structures within departments and agencies which contain evaluation staff and managers. The policy insists on relatively easy and direct access on the part of the evaluation unit head to the deputy.

Although much of the responsibility for program evaluation has been transferred to the OCG, the Treasury Board Secretariat maintains an involvement in a number of ways. The expenditure management process (PEMS) requires the submission of summaries of evaluations and departmental evaluation plans to the Treasury Board. The Treasury Board and the secretariats of the policy committees of the cabinet review departmental long-term and budget-year evaluation plans. Departmental requests for "new" money submitted to the Treasury Board and policy committees are required to include indications of how and when the new or "enhanced" activities are to be evaluated. They may direct that changes be made. In addition, all findings of evaluations of regulatory programs are supposed to be submitted to the Cabinet Committee on Regulations. To a considerable extent, the Treasury Board has made an effort to ensure that program evaluation considerations are built into the expenditure management process.

The policy committees of the cabinet, and particularly their secretariats, have additional responsibilities insofar as program evaluation is concerned. They may call for evaluation of programs of particular interest to groups of ministers. Although they are not the clients of evaluation studies, policy committees are potentially the most important users of such studies.

The Auditor General's Act, which was referred to above, allows (requires) value-for-money concerns — economy, efficiency, and effectiveness — to be applied by the auditor general's staff in auditing departments. The audit of the evaluation function, therefore, allows the auditor general to comment quite freely and extensively on the capacity and/or quality of evaluation capability and studies within departments. A formal audit described in the 1983 *Report of the Auditor General* (Canada annual) indicated major improvements during the 1978–1983 period. A subsequent audit discussed in the 1986 *Report* commented favorably on the improvements in the methodological quality of recent evaluations.

The structural aspects of the program evaluation policy are not unusual in Canada. Central agencies, especially the OCG in this case, often have the control and service functions so aptly described by Drucker. An external control is provided by the auditor general, and his influence is considerable. The creation of distinct structures within departments and the insistence on access to the deputy head reinforces the importance attached to the function. The deputy head responsibility reflects a management philosophy thoroughly discussed by the Lambert Commission. The inclusion of evaluation activities within the expenditure-management process reflects the restraint pressures experienced by government.

What is somewhat more problematic is the accountability element insofar as ministerial responsibility and the role of Parliament are concerned. Reforms which affect the powers and operation of committees of the House of Commons and the application of access-to-information legislation may well conflict with traditional understandings of the relationship between public servants and elected ministers and between the cabinet and the legislature. The issue of accountability and accountability relationships is one of the more important aspects of the review of evaluation policy which is currently underway within the OCG. At the present time, it is difficult to determine what decisions may be taken to enhance the accountability objects of program evaluation within the government of Canada. The recent development of the Improved Management Accountability (IMA) system does suggest an enhanced responsibility for senior line managers to ensure that serious evaluations of the programs for which they are responsible are undertaken and that there are appropriate policy and operational responses to the results of such studies.

The central role of the Treasury Board Secretariat in the creation of IMA also indicates that this central agency will be exercising close supervision over the extent to which departments implement the new scheme. At the same time, it must be noted that the pressures of fiscal restraint, when coupled with preoccupations with productivity and efficiency concerns, may reinforce the tendency, noted by the Neilson Task Force, of managers to reduce program evaluations to major examinations of operational issues related to the ongoing administration of programs within departments. The refusal of the prime minister in 1987 to increase access to government documents suggests that the government is hesitant to take steps which might politicize further the program evaluation process in Canada. It does appear, however, that the evaluation process, although subject to modification, will remain largely intact.

The Evaluation Process

Figure 1.2 provides a model of the evaluation process in Canada. It is conceptually straightforward, but practically complex. The process consists of seven largely sequential steps which range from the development of policy to the preparation and submission of evaluation reports.

All departments and agencies are required to develop evaluation policies which are compatible with Treasury Board policy. The departmental policy is expected to be comprehensive. It should outline the organizational aspects, roles, responsibilities, and accountability of officers involved. It will describe procedures for carrying out evaluations and for decision making based on findings. In addition, departmental policy must demonstrate a commitment to include line management in the program evaluation process. The resulting document, which contains detailed commitments on resource allocation and information flows, is submitted to the OCG. The OCG has a responsibility to examine, comment upon, and, if necessary, require amendments to the evaluation policy proposals submitted by departments. The OCG has agreed to provide assistance and expertise to departments requesting aid in the development of acceptable policies. It is useful to note that although ten basic elements are expected to be included in such policy statements, departments have an opportunity to use discretion and to develop structures, processes, and reporting relationships that they feel are best suited to departmental needs. The Treasury Board policy, while restrictive, does allow some flexibility for departments to determine the means they deem most useful for the conduct of program evaluations. The responsibility of the OCG

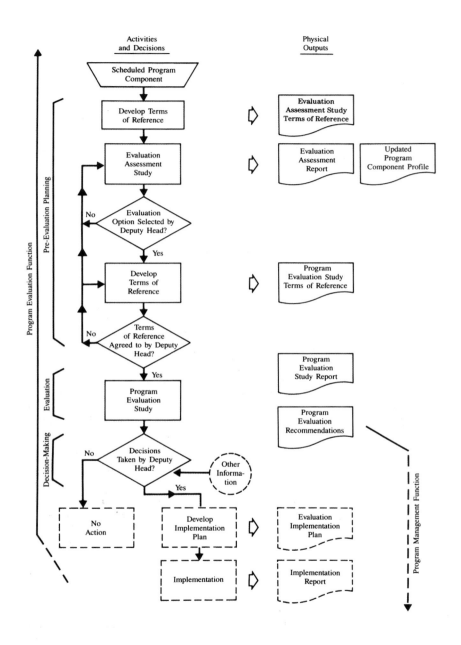

FIGURE 1.2
The Program Evaluation Process: A Representative Model

30

review is to ensure that the policy statements meet established requirements, are logical and internally consistent, and are capable of being implemented. The potential conflict between the service and control functions of the OCG is real; however, experience suggests that approval of departmental policies has taken place without frequent and serious battles with the central agency.

The departmental policy establishes the framework within which departmental evaluation activities must take place. Once the policy is in place, the necessary planning process begins.

Departments have a responsibility to prepare, submit, defend and, if necessary, amend evaluation plans. The plan is, in fact, two interrelated plans. The first is a long-term evaluation strategy which contains two elements — a program evaluation profile and a program evaluation schedule. The second is a plan of evaluation activities proposed for the upcoming fiscal year. It is logically the most detailed part of the overall department evaluation plan.

The planning process is a demanding one. Departments are required to arrange programs into appropriate groupings, referred to as program evaluation components. In addition, priorities have to be assigned to components so that an evaluation cycle can be produced. The deputy's role in this process is important. "As the client of the evaluation studies, he or she should determine what is to be evaluated and when" (*Guide*, PEB 1981a, 38).

Defining program components is not always easy. Activities of the department must be linked together logically so that they relate to a common objective that is a focus of concern for the deputy. They are "seen to be impacts — and effects-oriented, typically built around the intended effects of the department's or agency's activities" (*Guide*, PEB 1981a, 41). This means that they may not coincide perfectly with departmental structure. Discretion remains in the hands of the deputy on this issue.

Once the components have been identified, component profiles must be prepared. These profiles deal with two major topics — background, and elements and structure. The former refers to statements regarding mandate, objective(s) description, and the relationship with estimates and resources. The latter deals with activities, outputs, expected outcomes (impacts and effects), and the structure(s) involved.

When satisfactory profiles have been developed, the evaluation cycle may be prepared. This priority-setting exercise is based upon two major factors. The first is the importance of component evaluation insofar as the department is concerned. The second is the priority indicated by cabinet committees. As indicated previously, the two factors may not always be compatible and adjustments may be required if the Treasury Board and the policy committees insist.

Within the context of the department's overall evaluation plan, an annual plan must be prepared and submitted as part of the estimates process. This more detailed submission should

- identify which components will be evaluated;
- describe the timing of major elements of the evaluation process;
- outline the human and financial resource requirements;
- indicate who will carry out the work;
- update relevant component profiles.

The approval of evaluation plans does not mean that all program evaluation planning requirements have been completed.

Evaluation plans refer and apply to existing programs operated by departments. New and/or renewed programs face a somewhat different route, which has a similar purpose in mind. In this latter case, evaluation considerations must be built into program-proposal submissions which ultimately will require cabinet approval. This means the inclusion of an evaluation framework. The evaluation framework is designed to assist in the provision of appropriate data and evaluation questions for subsequent evaluation studies. By ensuring that such questions are addressed in the development and implementation of new or renewed programs, it is expected that evaluation studies will be conducted more efficiently and will meet appropriate quality standards more fully.

Once the planning requirements have been met and approved, evaluation per se begins. In the government of Canada, this involves four major steps — an evaluability assessment, the development of acceptable terms of reference for the evaluation study, the study itself, and the evaluation report and follow-up.

Evaluation assessment is an important part of the preparation required for the conduct of an evaluation. It may in fact outline a number of reasons supporting a recommendation that an evaluation be postponed. The basic purpose of the evaluation study is to ensure that appropriate terms of reference can be developed for each evaluation study. As such, it should outline the major issues to be addressed (evaluation questions) and recommend specific methodologies appropriate to respond to such questions.

The terms of reference define precisely what the evaluation study will do and how it will be conducted, provide the necessary authority, and specify the resources allocated to the study. This means that the specific evaluation questions will be stated. In addition, methodologies, criteria, information requirements, personnel, timetabling, and reporting will be described in considerable detail.

These terms of reference, which require approval by the deputy head, provide direction and a basis for assessing the extent to which the work completed meets original requirements. They become particularly important in cases where outside consultants are employed to conduct the study.

It is fair to state that the preference within the public service of Canada is that evaluations be carried out by appropriate staff within the department: staff who have the necessary analytical and methodological as well as interpersonal skills required for each study. The policy recognizes that, on occasion, the services of outside consultants may have to be utilized. Because of the more arm's-length relationship between consultants and senior departmental management, the *Guide* places great emphasis on the need to provide very elaborate terms of reference for such situations. In addition, it is strongly suggested that program-evaluation-unit personnel maintain frequent and effective links with the consultant to ensure that the deputy head is fully informed of proposed changes to, or difficulties encountered during, the conduct of the evaluation.

If the pre-evaluation planning activities have been conducted properly and if a thorough evaluation assessment report has been submitted, the evaluation study should be a relatively straightforward exercise. In practice, however, such studies operate under a number of constraints. These may include a lack of time, insufficient staff or financial resources, and, more frequently, methodological concerns that affect the reliability and validity of conclusions.

In principle, a series of steps is involved in any evaluation study. Information necessary to respond to the evaluation questions must be collected and organized in an appropriate manner. The data must be analyzed using proper techniques. On that basis, conclusions regarding the evaluation questions should become obvious. Finally, recommendations for decisions are prepared.

In practice, it is not always possible to apply techniques or obtain data that allow one to produce definitive conclusions. What evaluators attempt to do is to obtain the best evidence available within the constraints imposed and apply sound judgement in formulating conclusions and recommendations. Such limitations to the quality of evaluation studies are understood and permitted in Canada. Nonetheless, it is expected that all evaluations will

- address relevant and significant questions;
- yield credible findings and recommendations;
- be cost-justified. (*Principles* 1981)

The issue of methodological approach and quality is one which concerns both internal and external observers (Rayner 1986). At the present time, a basic response is to ensure that these concerns are dealt with in the evaluation report.

Principles suggests that evaluation reports should contain six sections or chapters. The first is the customary executive summary. The introduction contains a component profile, a description of the evaluation questions posed, and an indication of significant constraints under which the study was conducted. The third section describes the methodologies and indicators used by the evaluation team. A summary of the analyses carried out indicates the procedures used to ensure the reliability and accuracy of the data (information) collected and used. The evaluation findings chapter provides the conclusions of the study; it contains the answers to the evaluation questions posed and recommendations for action where appropriate. Finally, most evaluation reports contain technical appendices which are most useful for assessments of the propriety of the methodologies employed.

These reports are submitted to the deputy head for consideration and frequently for decision. Other users such as the cabinet, cabinet committees, and individual ministers may also receive copies of evaluation reports. At this stage, it is expected that some response to the evaluation study will be taken. There is evidence that suggests that evaluation reports do not merely gather dust. Some policy changes have resulted from the operation of the program evaluation function within departments. For example, as a result of an evaluation, the Canadian Home Insulation Program was revised to improve its cost-effectiveness. A more extreme case involved the ENERGUIDE Program. Prior to the evaluation, the Department of Consumer and Corporate Affairs had planned to renew and extend this program. The evaluation study led to the conclusion that the program should be terminated. More frequently, operational revisions are introduced to facilitate more cost-effective means of delivery of departmental programs (Rayner 1986).

Conclusion

This description of the program evaluation function in the government of Canada was undertaken to allow a response to a series of questions. Policy evaluation is initiated by the deputy heads of government departments and agencies within the parameters established by Treasury Board policy on program evaluation. Evaluation activities, plans, reports, and units are subject to assessment and more formal evaluation by the OCG, the Treasury Board and policy committees of the cabinet, and the auditor general of Canada. Most evaluation studies are conducted by departmental evaluation staff and line managers, although outside consultants may be employed as part of the evaluation team. The costs of evaluation are borne by the department. The report suggested by the PEB is extensive and has been described above. The deputy head, central agencies, and cabinet committees use reports. In addition, interest groups, parliamentarians, academics, and the media may be given access to such reports within the framework established by the Access to Information Act.

Program evaluation in the government of Canada has developed significantly since the 1977 policy statement was formulated. A key step was the creation of the PEB within the OCG. The function is ongoing and comprehensive in scope. It is an approach which attempted to avoid errors of the past and to respond to current conditions and needs. It is also a process and policy under considerable scrutiny from within and without. In the mid-1980s, approximately one hundred formal evaluation studies were conducted each year. Rayner (1986) estimated that the government of Canada must double its evaluation output if it wishes to approach the targets suggested by the Royal Commission on Financial Management and Accountability. To date, efforts to increase the commitment of resources to program and policy evaluation have been seriously limited by the budgetary restraint policies of the government. Experience under the new policy indicates a number of shortcomings which have emerged during the decade. The same experience also demonstrates how much the program evaluation function has developed and improved during this period.

I am indebted to Dr. John Mayne, Assistant Director of the Policy Division, Program Evaluation Branch, Office of the Comptroller General, and to Dr. Ray Rist, Deputy Director, General Government Division, United States General Accounting Office for their helpful comments on an earlier draft of this paper. Responsibility for all errors, of course, rests with the author.

References

Adie, R., and P. Thomas. 1982. *Canadian public administration: Problematical perspectives.* Scarborough: Prentice-Hall.

Canada. annual. *Report of the auditor general.* Ottawa: Supply and Services.

Canada, Royal Commission on Financial Management and Accountability (Lambert Commission). 1979. *Final report.* Ottawa: Supply and Services.

Canada, Royal Commission on Government Organization (Glassco Commission). 1962–63. *Reports.* Ottawa: Queen's Printer.

Davidson, G. F. 1966. *Financial Management.* Ottawa: Treasury Board.

Dobell, R., and D. Zussman. 1981. "An evaluation system for government: If politics is theatre then evaluation is (mostly) art." *Canadian Public Administration* 24 (3).

Doern, G., and A. Maslove. 1979. "The public evaluation of government spending: From methods to incentives." in *The Public Evaluation of Government Spending*, G. B. Doern and A. Maslove, eds. Montreal: Institute for Research on Public Policy.

Doerr, A. 1981. *The machinery of government.* Toronto: Macmillan.

Drucker, P. 1954. *The practice of management.* New York: Harper & Row.

Drury, C. M. 1969. *Planning programming budgeting guide.* rev. ed. Ottawa: Information Canada.

Jordan, J., and S. Sutherland. 1979. "Assessing the results of public expenditure: Program evaluation in the Canadian federal government." *Canadian Public Administration* 22 (4).

McNamara, E. F. 1979. "The outlook for program evaluation in the Canadian federal government." in International Conference on the Future of Public Administration, *Conference Proceedings* 7. Quebec City: ENAP.

Office of the Comptroller General. 1980. *Program evaluation: A discussion.* Ottawa: Office of the Comptroller General.

Prince, M. 1979. "Policy advisory groups in government departments." in *Public policy in Canada: Organization process and management*, G. B. Doern and P. Aucoin eds. Toronto: Macmillan.

Program Evaluation Branch. 1985. *Background notes for seminar on program evaluation: What's new after twenty years.* Ottawa: Office of the Comptroller General of Canada.

Program Evaluation Branch, Office of the Comptroller General. 1981a. *Guide on the Program Evaluation Functions.* Ottawa: Supply and Services.

Program Evaluation Branch, Office of the Comptroller General. 1981b. *Principles for the Evaluation of Programs by Federal Departments and Agencies.* Ottawa: Supply and Services.

Rayner, M. 1986. "Using evaluation in the federal government." *Canadian Journal of Program Evaluation* 1 (1).

Rogers, H. November 1979. "The changing environment for program evaluation." Address to a workshop on managing the program evaluation function.

_____. April 1979. "Program evaluation and its role in management of the federal public service." Notes for an address to the Management Consulting Institute Workshop on Program Evaluation.

Treasury Board of Canada. 1977. Circular No. 1977-47. Ottawa: Secretary of the Treasury Board.

2

Program Evaluation in the Federal Republic of Germany

Hans-Ulrich Derlien

Introduction

Program evaluation (PE), although sometimes traced back to the 1930s (Freeman 1977, 18), is a product of reform policies of the 1960s. The term was coined and the methodology refined predominantly in the United States. The idea mushroomed in the European countries, including the Federal Republic of Germany (FRG) in the late 1960s.

PE can be regarded as an instrumental — as opposed to social, political, or juridical — feedback mechanism, by which politics and administration can judge program performance. It is usually defined as the systematic (that is, employing scientific methods) investigation of the effectiveness and the actual effects (foreseen and unforeseen, intended and unintended) of public intervention programs (Weiss 1972). It is generally accepted that the need for systematic policy making (Dror 1968), ex ante and ex post, increases as the politico-administrative system shifts from primarily reactive towards a predominantly proactive strategy of governing.

Traditional budgetary feedback mechanisms and monitoring procedures are bound to fall short of meeting the functional requirements of a proactive policy conceived as a rational intervention into the economic and social processes and structures of a society. As commonly used, they would not provide information on (1) whether program goals had been met or not, (2) whether positive or negative side effects or spillovers had occurred, (3) what the causes of program failures might have been, and (4) how programs could possibly be amended.

These limitations on conventional information systems provide sound

37

reasons for establishing PE as a regular function in the process of managing public affairs. This is particularly so with innovative reform programs and even social experiments where there is uncertainty about their impacts and effectiveness. Uncertainty due to a change from incremental towards innovative and comprehensive planning is further enhanced if the programs cannot be logically derived from and the effects predicted on the grounds of a valid scientific theory of the particular policy area. The less the prediction of results can be accomplished and the less that cost-benefit analysis can be employed, the greater the need for ex post evaluation. Otherwise, sound information on the program, pre or post, is not to be had.

The Evolution of Program Evaluation in the Federal Bureaucracy

In the first years of PE, the more the importance given to planned intervention, the more the quality of policy analysis changed as well. Planning staffs, social indicators and statistics in general, forecasting, cost-benefit analysis, electronic data processing, and evaluation were all gradually established in Bonn after the establishment of the reformist social-liberal coalition government in 1969 (Schatz 1973; Bebermeyer 1974). Following the logic of the policy cycle, PE was eventually institutionalized and practiced with a certain time lag after the first wave of reform legislations had been launched.

Second, apart from the increased demand for scientific information in general and for evaluative data in particular, the development of PE subsequent to enforced planning activities was brought about by an increased need for reallocating financial capacities from ineffective to effective programs. As reform policies normally face financial restrictions, there is an additional need to legitimate new expenditures and the curbing of old programs, or both, by proving them to be effective or ineffective, respectively.

Information, allocation, and legitimation were the arguments by which the institutionalization of PE was claimed and justified by those advocating a rational policy-making process. The actual motives, however, varied from parliamentary pressures and budgetary enforcements to public criticism of existing programs, internal administrative politics, and predispositions of bureaucratic culture to co-opt new sources of information.

At present, as the individual ministries are relatively autonomous in shaping their internal structure, the degree of specialization of the evaluation function varies strongly from ministry to ministry. The picture is rather scattered, in addition, as the terminology used to describe the evaluation function is not a unitary one.

It is hard, therefore, to tell whether and to what extent there is a difference between sections specializing in evaluation and those concerned with "statistics," "research," "reports to parliament," "cost-benefit analysis," "macroeconomic studies," or "information systems." After all, those sections overtly involved in substantive policy questions very often have vague titles or titles only suggesting budgetary interests, all the while conducting key research studies. I shall, therefore, ignore titles and concentrate on those evaluation settings which are formally institutionalized and which have documented instances of conducting public-sector program evaluations.

There are basically three arenas in which PE is found at the federal level in the FRG:

- institutionalization of special evaluation units in individual ministries;
- institutionalization of PE with specific legislated programs;
- institutionalization of PE with social experiments.

Evaluation units. PE involves socioeconomic research and therefore requires know-how that is not easily available in the traditional juridically trained federal bureaucracy. Therefore, some of the departments which must relatively often carry out evaluations have established special units for this task. This is not to suggest that the evaluation proper is carried through by administrative personnel. On the contrary, it is regularly accomplished by commissioned research. But the ministries need specialists for discussing research designs, providing data, keeping contact with the external research team, commenting on the research report, and, last but not least, contracting potential researchers.

In the case of the FRG an additional cause has contributed to the evolution of evaluation units in some of the departments. In the 1969 budget-reform legislation, cost-benefit analyses were prescribed and could be required by the Ministry of Finance in preparing future budgets (Derlien 1978). Those ministries with big budgets containing large investment programs were exposed to intense accountability pressures. One means of responding was to establish these new units. For example:

- The Ministry of Agriculture, with its huge subsidy programs, in 1973 changed its organization structure to parallel its programs. Subsequently, it institutionalized a section in the planning unit in order to specialize in ex ante and ex post analyses. PE of a less-sophisticated nature is regularly required by the program units to justify their budget proposals within the department.
- The Ministry of Transport initially created a section for cost-benefit analysis in its planning unit in 1970. It extended the tasks of this section to incorporate ex post evaluations in 1978. Furthermore, in one of the

agencies of the ministry concerned with federal roads, there were also specialists occupied with the evaluation of a number of safety regulations, particularly of experiments with speed limitations (1971).

- The Ministry of Developmental Aid was the first ministry to establish an evaluation unit to survey its developmental projects — not so much for budgetary reasons, but rather because of particular political needs and because of the longer tradition evaluation has had internationally in this policy area. To a certain extent it was also parliamentary pressure on the ministry that led it to have this unit in 1970.
- Also due to prolonged parliamentary pressure (1968–1974) the Ministry of Technology instituted an evaluation unit. But in contrast to other units noted here, it is less engaged in impact research and, rather, more in reviewing research institutions and the implementation of funded projects.
- Information programs have been evaluated by special staffs in the Federal Agency for Press Relations since 1968 and in the Federal Agency for Health Information since 1974.

The structural differentiation and specialization of the evaluation function was brought about by the frequency with which evaluative reports were required by the Ministry of Finance and by the Parliament. There were also needs for such information in the ministries because of their other planning responsibilities. The cases reveal that the focus of evaluation is on the departmental level of government. Central political and administrative institutions do not play an active role, even in 1989.

- Since 1969 the Chancellor's Office has had in its planning division a section which specialized in planning techniques and setting "priorities and posteriorities." Only after the change in government in 1982 did the emphasis on evaluation become more explicit, when the respective task was called "implementation assessment of government programs." This however, does not mean that the Bundeskanzleramt has been or is now particularly involved in specific evaluations (see the subsection "Distribution of Functions in the Evaluation Process" in this chapter). It merely claims a stake in the process and occasionally surveys departmental evaluation activities (König 1986).
- Interestingly enough, the Federal Accounting Office (Bundesrechnungshof, BRH), although legally obliged to check organizations as to their effectiveness, has abstained from engaging in PE. Traditional role understanding emphasizing cost containment and compliance to budgetary regulations (Tiemann 1974; Schäfer 1977), together with a neutral, nonpartisan position in politics, which would conflict with any assessment of (policy) goal achievement (Battis 1976), as well as the training of its staff, have contributed to the fact that the responsibility for PE, so far, has remained exclusively in the executive branch. Recently, how-

ever, the BRH has slightly changed its position (Wittrock 1986; Zavelberg 1986) by acknowledging PE as a possible, albeit exceptional, part of auditing. In fact, since 1985, the annual reports of the BRH contain results from evaluations. Furthermore, the BRH regards as one of its tasks the need to review the state of the art of PE in the federal government. A survey conducted in 1986 has, however, not yet been released.

- Federal Parliament institutionalized PE in a number of legislated programs (see below) and requests some two hundred regular reports from the executive branch. It has, though, neither enough staff capacity to digest the various reports nor the capacity and specialists to conduct studies on its own.

Evaluation of specific legislated programs. The German Parliament has played an important role in adapting its mechanisms of legislative and budgetary control to the new functional and complex requirements of planning. Uncertainty about the substantive impact and financial implications of new programs are the predominant motives for requiring programs to prove their effectiveness and efficiency. Apart from political agreements to evaluate individual programs, Parliament (after 1969) increasingly required the federal government to report on implementation and impacts of specific programs by mandating evaluations in the authorizing program legislation. Examples include

- joint federal-state program to improve the regional economic structure (1970),
- labor market and employment act (1969),
- law to continue the payment of wages in case of illness (1969),
- amendment of the social subsidies act (1969),
- hospital investment program (1971),
- postgraduate grants law (1970),
- general educational grants law (1969),
- legal abortion law (1975),
- legal protection of tenants against arbitrary notice (1971),
- various reports on subsidies and taxes (1970 to present).

Evaluation of experimental policy. A special type of reform policy consists of carrying through social experiments. Of course, experiments logically imply the necessity of evaluating them in order to learn from their results, before general regulations are enacted. Experiments were initially carried out in housing construction in the mid 1960s (Bohnsack et al. 1977); later on the idea of experimental policy spread to other policy areas, in particular to education and health policy. These latter two areas are obviously "soft" policies to which PE is most suitable, but it was also for a political reason that the federal government started to carry out experiments under the label "model programs" in these areas: legislation in education and health is normally a task constitutionally assigned to the individual states. The federal government is merely authorized to regulate basic questions in so-called frame legislations. Thus, launching experiments was a way to practice reform policy on foreign territory and, second, to do it not with legislation, but by simple administrative (executive) agreements between federal and individual state governments. The justification for this arrangement was that experiences should be accumulated in order to clarify basic questions, which are within the jurisdiction of the federal government (Hellstern and Wollmann 1983).

The federal government has reported to Parliament (Bundestags (BT)-Drs. 9/699) that, between 1971 and 1980 in educational policy, 1,368 experiments, subsidized with DM 736 million have been carried out; another 166 experiments in university education and 225 in vocational training were financed with DM 143 million and DM 53 million, respectively. Very often, however, the evaluations in this area are in-house evaluations, at best standardized reports in the form of expert judgements. An exception to the rule were evaluations of experiments with comprehensive schools (Raschert 1974), a highly politicized issue in the 1970s.

The most prominent experimental program to be evaluated is the Humanization of Labor Program in the Ministry of Technology. Not only are the individual model projects evaluated, but the dissemination of their results in industry and administration is investigated as well. Furthermore, the ministry by 1988 (for the third time) invited evaluation experts to review the sub-programs.

PE on the Länder and Community Level

Although there is no survey available of the situation in the individual states of the federation, it may be generalized that the evaluation function has not developed as much as on the federal level. This proposition contradicts the hypothesis that there is a stress towards structural consistency of planning and evaluation, as the Länder (individual states) generally practice developmental and, in particular, regional planning. However, the Länder dispose of most of the German administrative field offices and rely on administrative monitoring.

At the community level, Volz (1980) found only six major cities which practice evaluations. Again, it is the direct political feedback to local policy makers which might sufficiently fulfill their informational needs.

Distribution of Functions in the Evaluation Process

The systematic ex post evaluations of experimental and reform policies is obviously a task which can hardly be accomplished by traditional external control institutions (Parliament, Federal Accounting Office) or the ministerial bureaucracy. Even those ministries with special evaluation units do not in general conduct the actual research work, that is, data collection and analysis. Evaluation research is basically external (commercial and academic), commissioned research.

The question should be asked, which functions in the evaluation process can be attributed to the political and administrative institutions on the federal level (Derlien 1978b). In an ideal-typical way the scenery can be depicted as follows: PE is primarily initiated by Parliament and in a rather ad hoc fashion by the departments in charge of a program. The primary function of the departments and their sections is to administer the external evaluation research and to write parliamentary reports on the basis of the evaluation studies, including suggestions for program amendments.

The relative decentralization of the evaluation function to the departmental level can be explained structurally. First, the corresponding planning functions are also not centralized in the FRG: the Chancellor's Office, rather, confines itself to coordinating functions (Dyson 1975). Second, this decentralization is supported by the Constitution, which gives the individual ministries a good deal of autonomy in initiating and executing their policies, whereas the cabinet is merely involved in programs to be submitted to legislation and in fundamental policy questions. Departmental autonomy is particularly large in coalition governments with the ministers of one or the other fraction being in a veto position. Centralizing planning and evaluation in the Ministry of Finance as an alternative would not be meaningful in the FRG, because budgeting and planning are not integrated, but follow the traditional two-track system.

A separate evaluation office has recently been recommended (Reding 1981), but certainly will not be institutionalized in addition to the Federal Accounting Office.

Imbalance in the Evaluation of Policies

From what has been reported so far, it should be clear that PE, even on the federal level, is far from covering all policy areas. It is closely linked to the fields of education, health, housing, and social affairs. This, however, means that new programs in these areas have been under particular pressure to prove themselves effective, whereas "old" policies, in particular subsidies in economic and agricultural policy, are not scrutinized.

Second, "hard" policies, for example, technology policy or infrastructural projects (highways and canals), are judged on the basis of ex ante cost-benefit analyses, with their somewhat shaky methodology. Reliance on predictability of effects and calculability of benefits and even monetary costs, for instance of nuclear power plants, has, however, increasingly been undermined in recent years. In 1981, the parliamentary Committee for Technology Policy has organized a group of experts into a subcommittee to carry out technology assessments (BT-Drs. 9/701 29:7, 1981; Böhret and Franz 1982).

Apart from differences in the applicability of PE in the various policy areas, there are psychological obstacles to further institutionalization of PE. Evaluation is normally regarded by practitioners as a monitoring procedure, and this is in accordance with its rationale as a management tool. But as in the FRG, PE often is described in traditional control terminology, for example, *"Erfolgskontrolle,"* or "Inspection"; it is associated with person-oriented performance measurements or juridical controls of individual decisions. Program failures, thus, tend to be personalized and interpreted by administrators in terms of guilt and responsibility instead of cause and effect. Furthermore, there are additional obstacles when the evaluation function is not located in special and organizationally separate units. Initiating the evaluation of a program by the person in charge would mean to a minister or section head not only the possibility of incurring negative political or administrative sanctions, but also cognitive dissonances if the program did not produce the expected (and promised!) results. As Nienaber and Wildavsky have put it: "Is evaluative man a kind of official eunuch who has no feeling about the programs he runs?" (Nienaber and Wildavsky 1973, 6). Unless legally instituted, considerable public scrutiny and even criticism will be needed in order to induce an ad hoc evaluation. Resistance against PE will be the stronger when the program is firmly entrenched. Vested interests of program beneficiaries and the self-confidence of the administration tend to neglect or deflect all criticisms.

Sunset Legislation

The automatic termination of a program, unless its effectiveness has been proved (Bothun and Comer 1979; Adams and Sherman 1978), is regarded in the United States as a means to make the executive branch more inclined to have PE carried through. It can be interpreted as a special mode to enforce PE legislatively. Although there are serious doubts in this country as to whether sunset legislation is compatible with constitutional law, it has been practiced with the Second Law on Protection of Tenants against Arbitrary Notice 1974, the evaluation report being published in 1979 (BT-Drs. 8/2610). Furthermore, the conservative-liberal government, which had come to power in 1982, announced that a regulation which forces clients to share costs of hospital treatment was to be evaluated in 1984. The above-mentioned social experiments with comprehensive schools and juridical training were also terminated.

In Rhineland-Palatium, generally all administrative regulations and circulars expire after five years (Kindermann 1981, 60). This device, however, was taken less with respect to PE than as a measure to initiate debureaucratization and deregulation.

Boobytraps and Pitfalls

There are, however, also reasons inherent to evaluation methodology and lessons from the politics of evaluation which might explain why the federal bureaucracy is not particularly keen on institutionalizing an evaluation system on a broader scale. As the administration in Bonn hesitated in the late 1960s to readily copy foreign integrated planning and budgeting systems like the planning, programming, and budgeting (PPB) system or Rationalisation des Choix Budgetaines (RCB), the present administration also seems to have had a certain skepticism about the purely technical feasibility of PE.

The Iron Law of Evaluation Flaws

In order to function properly, PE has to cope with a number of methodological problems which are quite characteristic for this type of applied research. Meanwhile there are many U.S. textbooks on the methodology of evaluation research, which do not fail to take account of these specific problems. Practitioners speak of the "iron law of evaluation flaws" (Williams 1971, 123). I have shown elsewhere (Derlien 1976) that these problems were faced in Bonn, too.

Operationalizing Goals

Normally the methodological presuppositions of PE are not met by a program to be evaluated. Some programs do not have explicit goal descriptions; others do have goal descriptions, but are too ambitious to be ever accomplished. Still others are too ambiguously formulated or are informationally empty. There are often political reasons for this lack of precision in formulating program goals: formulations referring to general welfare and happiness of the majority are likely to secure political support, as the electorate can interpret them arbitrarily and believe that individual expectations will be met. The more ambiguous and the less operational goal descriptions actually are, the easier is political consensus building (Braybrooke and Lindblom 1963). Some programs might even be launched for symbolic purposes with no specific effects to be achieved at all (Edelman 1964).

As a consequence of political bargaining, goals are formulated in an abstract way in order to disguise basic political controversies. The solution to these ambiguities is, sometimes intentionally, deferred into the implementation process. Because of these political functions of goal formulations, they are regularly not formulated in precise terms at the beginning, but rather at the end of the policy process.

Furthermore, when it is possible to derive indicators of goal achievement, they tend to measure only the positive and intended effects of a program. These are the effects that are of political interest, if only because it was these stated effects that warranted the political support. Difficult and risky as it may be, unforeseen positive and negative impacts should be investigated as well.

Facing this situation the researcher is bound to be selective in measuring the impact of a program. He is also likely to stimulate political conflicts when trying to specify what might have been (positively or negatively) expected by program proponents and opponents. Case studies show that evaluation research that sticks to goal formulations and tries to operationalize them without taking into account the various and often-conflicting political expectations, or that is too selective in investigating unforeseen consequences, does not succeed in being politically accepted afterwards. It is blamed for not having measured what the program under scrutiny had intended to achieve. The blame can also be for the reverse—neglecting negative side effects which emerged since the program was implemented.

Design Problems

Apart from other methodological problems, for example, flaws in data collection, there is, second, the problem of causal inference, as the methodological ideal of an experimental design can hardly be accomplished. In Germany, many programs are legislated and therefore cannot be withheld from a control group. Social experiments are thus mostly quasi-experimental. Therefore, systematic variation of program elements in order to learn about the relative effectiveness and efficiency of alternative program designs is hardly realized. Other influences also impact on the design. For example:

- The geographical location often is the result of a political decision rather than of systematically striving for representativeness.
- The program variables are not kept constant, as for instance in school experiments where teachers would not wait to improve situations until the research results were published.
- There is no random sampling of those participating, for instance, in a school experiment. Hawthorne effects, that is, self-fulfilling prophecies, are likely when the most highly motivated teachers and children as well as parents in favor of comprehensive schools recruit themselves into the experiment (AuClaire 1977).

Evaluation practice facing these problems increasingly seems to lower its methodological level of aspiration. Evaluators recognize that programs are not logically derived from specified goals and are not experimentally designed before being enacted as a law. Thus the policy process does not follow the Popperian methodology of falsification and modification of policy theories. This situation, consequently, contributed to the growing acceptance of qualitative research methods and quasi-experimental designs not just as a second best way, but as the only adequate procedure. It is difficult to judge, in the end, where methodological prostitution starts, particularly in commissioned research. Sacrificing methodological standards can, after all, devalue the use of research in the policy process. Nevertheless, the suggestion to check the evaluability of programs before an evaluation proper is done (Wholey 1976) has hardly been taken up in the FRG.

Politicization of Evaluation Results

With externally ad hoc–initiated evaluations, the likelihood of negative results is relatively great, as there is always some truth in political feedback mechanisms. Past experience of this sort seems to have conditioned the basically defensive attitude of program administrators. It is not unusual if the research process is negatively affected by opposition and defensiveness on the part of those in charge of a program. The end result is increased methodological difficulties for the external evaluators, as cooperation in giving access to files and data may be lacking.

Negative evaluation results constitute a threat to the legitimacy of an ongoing program, the political success of a minister, and the administrative career of the official. In this situation the normal reaction is to question the validity of the research results. Be it that the methodological weaknesses are evident, be it that external counter-advice is asked for, the iron law of evaluation flaws offers lots of possibilities by which to maintain that the inefficiency of a program has not been validly demonstrated. Even in a field like regional policy evaluation, carried out predominantly by economists, there is serious methodological infighting as to the validity of the findings (Krist and Nicol 1982).

An outstanding example in the FRG of the tendency to politicize evaluation results (Weiss 1970) is the interpretation of the comprehensive school experiments by advocates and opponents of this school type (Raschert 1981). On the other hand, in the case of the Humanization of Labor Program, evaluation is not politicized, since the federal government had promised the labor unions not to put the program into question whatever the evaluation results might reveal.

Research Utilization

In recent years evaluation researchers and policy analysts in general seem to be increasingly concerned that their studies be utilized by administrators (Patton 1978; Wildavsky 1979). On the one hand the shaky state of the methodological art of practical evaluation studies has to be acknowledged (Bernstein and Freeman 1975; Cook and Gruder 1979). On the other hand, program administrators are blamed (implicitly, as I have done in the preceding paragraph) and said to behave irresponsibly if they do not take immediate decisions based on commissioned scientific "evidence." It has to be admitted that many studies (for whatever reason) contain methodological weaknesses. Meta-evaluation research should, therefore, extend its scope to isolate additional variables affecting the process of giving scientific advice, above all on qualitative aspects of the contents of research reports (Van de Vall and Bolas 1980) and on the information needs of administrators (Barkdoll 1980).

Perspectives

The German experience with PE, which is quite in line with findings elsewhere, indicates two new trends in policy studies. One trend concerns the administration of programs and the other, the professional evaluator.

As the possibility of taking action is so important for the political reception of a study, much more emphasis has been put on implementation studies in the late 1970s (Mayntz 1980). Such studies reveal failures which can be amended in a relatively short time. Further, these changes can be carried out quite soon after the program is launched. In contrast, impact evaluations necessarily can be carried out only after years of operation, because results will not be observable earlier.

Obviously, the time perspective of administrators is limited. If implementation studies gain importance therefore, it is only logical to save time by simulating the implementation process. This has been done in the FRG with respect to the effects of a program, particularly with new tax regulations and changes of the health and social insurance system. In addition, the implementation process, too, was simulated in the cases of the City Planning Law (1971), Building Regulation Law (1973, 1975) and the Youth Protection Law (1977) (Böhret and Hugger 1980).

The analogy between Popper's methodology of falsification as a rule for accumulating scientific knowledge and evaluation as a mechanism for improving programs seems to have led professional evaluators to believe in a rational model as opposed to the normally incremental reality of the policy process (DeYoung and Conner 1982). Politicization threats and utilization problems could help to redefine the evaluator's role in politics. Accepting that research is just one factor in the decision-making process, research reports are increasingly not only subject to "truth tests," but also to "utility tests" (Weiss and Bucuvalas 1980).

This change in the understanding of PE's role at least helped make bearable the fact that PE played almost no role in the policies of retrenchment after the change in government in October 1982, when a conservative government took power after thirteen years of Social-Democrat rule. The new government, terminating and curbing reform programs of the previous government for fiscal reasons and on the grounds of adverse political convictions, did not seek the legitimation of scientific evidence. After all, Thomas Kuhn has shown that even science does not progress "scientifically" according to Popper's methodology of falsification, but is driven forward by paradigmatic revolutions.

The more surprising it might be, then, that the Kohl government has not tried to tear down the existing evaluation arrangements which were too closely related to Social-Democrat reform policies. Rather, the new conservative government attempted to employ them as elements in a strategy of de-bureaucratization and deregulation, and general withdrawal of the state from society. The degree to which they have been successful in these efforts will become increasingly clear in time. But for the present, the preliminary results suggest they have not wasted their time in trying.

References

Adams, B., and B. Sherman. 1978. "Sunset implementation: A positive partnership to make government work." *Public Administration Review* 38, 78–81.

AuClaire, P. A. 1977. "The limits of social experimentation." *Sociological Practice* 2, 24–37.

Barkdoll, G. L. 1980. "Type III evaluations: Consultation and consensus." *Public Administration Review* 40, 174–179.

Battis, U. 1976. "Rechnungshof und politik." *Die Öffentleche Verwaltung* 29, 721–27.

Bebermeyer, H. 1974. "Regieren ohne management?" Planung als Führungsinstrument moderner Regierungsarbeit. Stuttgart: Bonn Aktvell.

Bernstein, I. N., and H. E. Freeman. 1975. Academic and Entrepreneurial Research, New York: Russell Sage.

Böhret, C., and W. Hugger. 1980. *Der praxistest von gesetzentwürfen*. Baden-Baden: Nomos.

Böhret, C., and P. Franz. 1982. *Technologiefolgenabschätzung*. New York: Institutionelle und verfahrensmassige Lösungsansatze. Frankfurt/New York: Campus.

Bohnsack, R., et al. 1977. "Modelleinrichtungen in der sozialpolitik. Experimentelle reformverfahren im rahmen der jugendhilfe." *Bürgernahe Gestaltung der sozialen Umwelt*, F.-X. Kaufmann ed. 150–93. Meisenheim.

Bothun, D., and J. C. Comer. 1979. "The politics of termination: Concepts and process." *Policy Studies Journal* 7, 540–53.

Braybrooke, D., and C. E. Lindblom. 1963. *Strategy of Decision*. Policy Evaluation as a Social Process. Glencoe, N.Y.: Free Press.

Cook, T. D., and C. Gruder. 1979. "Metaevaluation research." *Evaluation Studies Review Annual* 4, 469–515.

Derlien, H.-U. 1976. "Die erfolgskontrolle staatlicher Planung." *Eine empirische untersuchung über organisation, methode und politik der programmevaluation*. Baden-Baden: Nomos.

———. 1978a. "Die Effizienz von Entscheidungs-instrumenten für die staatliche Ressourcenallokation — Versuch einer Evaluation von Entscheidungstechniken." H.-C. Pfohl and B. Rurup, eds. *Anwendungsprobleme moderner Planungsund Entscheidungstechniken, Materialien zur Betriebs und Volkswirtschaftslehre* 3, 311–26. Königstein: Hanstein.

———. 1978b. "Organisatorische Aspekte der Programmevaluation." *Verwaltung und Fortbildung* 6, 51–61.

D'Young, D. J., and R. F. Conner. 1982. "Evaluator preconceptions about organizational decision making." *Evaluation Review* 6, 431–40.

Dror, Y. 1968. *Public policymaking reexamined*. San Francisco: Chandler.

Dyson, K. H. F. 1975. "Improving policy-making in Bonn: Why the central planners failed." *Journal of Management Studies* 12, 157–74.

Edelman, M. 1964. *The symbolic uses of politics*. Urbana: University of Illinois Press.

Freeman, H. E. 1977. "The present status of evaluation research." *Evaluation Studies Review Annual* 2, 17–51.

Hellstern, G.-M., and H. Wollmann, ed. 1983. *Experimentelle Politik — Reformstrohfeuer oder Lernstrategie*. Bestandsaufnahme und Evaluierung. Opladen: Westdeut-scher Verlag.

Kindermann, H. 1981. "Neue Richtlinien zur Gesetzestechnik." *Die Öffentliche Verwaltung* 34, 855.

König, K. 1986. "Zur Evaluation Staatlicher Programme." Eichhorn, P. and Kortzfleisch, G., eds. *Erfolgskontrolle bei der Verausgabung öffentlicher Mittel*, 19–34. Baden-Baden: Nomos.

Krist, H., and W. R. Nicol. 1982. "Wirkungsanalysen in der Regionalpolitik. Ein britisch/deutscher Vergleich." *Raumforschung und Raumordnung* 40, 133–46.

Mayntz, R., ed. 1980. *Implementation politischer Programme*. Königstein: Athenäum.

Nienaber, J., and A. Wildavsky. 1973. *The Budgeting and Evaluation of Federal Recreation Programs or Money Doesn't Grow on Trees*. New York: Basic Books.

Patton, M. Q. 1978. *Utilization-focused evaluation*. Beverly Hills/London: Sage.

Raschert, J. 1974. *Gesamtschule: Ein gesellschaftliches Experiment*. Stuttgart: Klett.

―――. 1981. "Probleme der Evaluation von Modellversuchen am Beispiel des Gesamtschulmodells in Nordrhein-Westfalen." H.-U. Derlien ed. *Probleme der Methodik und der Rezeption von Programmforschung*, 55–72. Munchen: GfP.

Reding, K. 1981. *Die Effizienz staatlicher Aktivitaten. Probleme ihrer Messung und Kontrolle*. Baden-Baden: Nomos.

Schäfer, H. 1977. *Wer kontrolliert unsere Steuergelder? Finanzprüfung durch den Bundesrechnungshof*. Stuttgart: Bonn Abtuell.

Schatz, H. 1973. "Auf der Suche nach neuen Problemlösungsstrategien: Die Entwicklung der politischen Planung auf Bundesebene." R. Mayntz and F. W. Scharpf, eds. *Planungsorganisation* 9–67. München: Piper.

Tiemann, S. 1974. *Die staatsrechtliche Stellung der Finanzkontrolle des Bundes*. Berlin: Duncker und Humblot.

Van de Vall, M., and C. Bolas. 1980. "Applied social discipline research of social policy research: The emergence of a professional paradigm in sociological research." *The American Sociologist* 128–37.

Volz, J. 1980. *Erfolgskontrolle kommunaler Planung. Eine Untersuchung uber Moglichkeiten und Grenzen der Erfolgskontrolle kommunaler Planungen*. Koln.

Weiss, C. H. 1970. "The politicization of evaluation research." *Journal of Social Issues* 26, 57–68.

―――. 1972. *Evaluation Research. Methods of Assessing Program Effectiveness*. Englewood Cliffs, N.J.: Prentice Hall.

Weiss, C. H., and M. J. Bucuvalas. 1980. "Truth tests and utility tests: Decision-makers' frames of reference for social science research." *American Sociological Review* 45, 302–13.

Wholey, J. S. 1976. "The role of evaluation and the evaluator in improving public programs: The bad news, the good news, and a bicentennial challenge." *Public Administration Review* 36, 679–83.

Wildavsky, A. 1979. *Speaking truth to power. The art and craft of policy analysis*. Boston: Little Brown.

Williams, W. 1971. *Social Policy Research and Analysis*. New York: Elsevier.

Wittrock, K. 1986. "Haushaltsgestaltung durch Finanzkontrolle." *Die Verwaltung* 19, 1–8.

Zavelberg, H.-G. 1986. "Staatliche Rechnungsprufungund Erfolgskontrolle. Moglichkeiten and Grenzen." Eichhorn and V. Kortzfleisch, eds. *Erfolgskontrolle bei der Verausgabung öffentlicher Mittel*, 103–20. Baden-Baden.

3

Policy Evaluation in British Government: From Idealism to Realism?

Bill Jenkins and Andrew Gray

Introduction

In 1983 Sir Douglas Wass, formerly permanent secretary in HM Treasury and the Joint Head of the British Civil Service, delivered a series of lectures on the ability of British central government to achieve what he defined as the vital twin objectives of efficiency and responsiveness. He began with an assessment of government's strategic capacity. "What I shall be doing," he explained, "is to look at the way our executive government is organized, at the mechanisms it uses to formulate its policies, and how it evaluates progress towards its objectives" (Wass 1983, 19).

Wass's assessment was not flattering: government mechanisms of strategic analysis and evaluation were at best strictly limited. In public expenditure decisions, especially, he saw little evidence of the application of any rational decision-making model. Indeed the major rules in British cabinet government could be encapsulated as: "Number one: as things have been then broadly so shall they remain," and "Number two: he who has the muscle gets the money" (Wass 1983, 21).

Wass argued that such a system could be defended only to a limited extent, for there was little in the way of policy analysis and evaluation. These were of prime importance in the business of government:

[I]t is surely right that policies should be rigorously evaluated and their effects set against objectives. Dependent as they are for political support on a public perception of their competence and resolve, it may be hard for governments to admit that they have been wrong. But without the strength of moral purpose to make such an admission they may in the long run expose themselves and the country to risks and dangers that far exceed the costs of a policy change. (Wass 1983, 21)

The above analysis is important not because it is necessarily the correct interpretation of past events but for the way it reflects what many have seen to be a muted commitment to policy evaluation by successive British governments. Yet even if true, is this a dated picture? In 1985 it was announced that in the future all papers going to the cabinet or cabinet committees that contained "value for money" implications would state what the proposals would achieve, by when, and at what cost. It would also be necessary to establish how improvement was going to be measured (Hogwood 1987, 244). As we will see, this commitment to evaluation is part of a wider movement to develop and cultivate a culture of financial management in British central and local government. Treasury officials now talk of policy evaluation as "a topical subject" (Butler 1986), while ministers extol the virtues of performance measurement and public sector management (MacGregor 1987).

To establish what has changed and the reality of the new commitment to policy evaluation this paper will first look briefly at the historical events of the 1960s and 1970s that provide the backdrop to Wass's doubts and reservations. It will then explore more recent developments in British central and local government (in particular the attempts to create a new climate of resource management) and, finally, assess the current state of policy evaluation in the United Kingdom (UK).

Policy Evaluation in the United Kingdom: A Little History

Constitutional and Administrative Background

In order to allow British experience in the field of policy evaluation to be compared with developments elsewhere, it is useful to sketch out some political and constitutional features of British government. Of particular note is the UK's parliamentary system, the complex nature of central-local government relations, and the fact that some services are administered centrally but delivered locally (for example, health).

Every elementary textbook on British politics describes how Britain has a cabinet government and ministers are responsible to Parliament. Exactly what these terms mean in the current day and age is less precise (Hennessy 1986). However, in theory at least, ministers can be held responsible for the actions of the departments they head (for example, agriculture, defense, health, and social security) and can be called to account to Parliament for departmental actions and programs. This can be done through the cut-and-thrust of parliamentary debate or through the activities of specialist select committees of the House of Commons. Indeed, one of the major constitutional functions of the latter is to scrutinize (evaluate?) the activities of the executive. Whether the House is capable of discharging this function and how far its powers really go is a matter of continued debate fanned recently by the affair of the Westland Helicopter Company and its aftermath (see, for example, Gray and Jenkins 1987).

The importance of the above for any discussion of policy evaluation is that policy programs are often perceived within government as ministerial rather than public property. As a consequence, evaluations may remain for internal governmental consumption enshrouded by the operations of the Official Secrets Act. Further, within this enclosed world the resource allocation battle continues between the spending departments and central agencies such as the Treasury. Information on programs is thus often a strategic resource useful in the trench warfare of the annual budgetary game. Here any demand for or use of evaluation may be motivated by political rather than managerial criteria as ideas of "collective responsibility" dissolve before a network of sectorial and partisan interests involving political and bureaucratic actors (Heclo and Wildavsky 1981).

The importance of such contextual factors will become clear below. So too will the fact that, while the UK is a unitary state, many policy functions are discharged or delivered not by central government but either by local government (housing, education) or by decentralized regional and district bodies (for example, health services, water resources). In the political climate of the late 1980s this map of public administration may be changing. However, at present it is necessary to be aware of the complex networks that characterize the world of central-local government relations. In the UK all local government powers derive from Parliament, yet local government remains the only elected tier of government away from Westminster. Local government is, therefore, a separate political form charged at the time of writing with delivering (in the context of central government policy) education, housing, social, and other services. For finance it remains heavily dependent on central grants, for it has little revenue-raising capacity of its own. However, local authorities see themselves as having their own mandates and being responsible to their own political constituencies. The potential effect of this on any "objective" evaluation by the center of services provided by the locality is a problematic issue we return to later.

The 1960s and 1970s: The Rise and
Fall of Rational Decision Making?

The passing love affair of governments with rational analysis, especially as captured by techniques such as planning, programming, and budgeting (PPB) and corporate planning, was a feature of many countries and many different levels of government in the 1960s. The UK was no exception, although in both central and local government the commitment to such techniques and approaches was never as full-blooded as elsewhere (for example, the United States), a fact reflected in the low allocation of political and administrative resources to such initiatives and a tendency to disengage rapidly from them when problems arose.

In the UK central government two main forces fueled an enthusiasm for policy analysis and evaluation in the late 1960s and early 1970s. The first of these, driven by the central bureaucracy, especially the Treasury, was a determination to install more effective mechanisms for controlling and prioritizing departmental spending decisions. The second force, rooted mainly in political initiatives, was for more management in government and more rational and collective decision making at the center (that is, the cabinet).

The origins and development of these initiatives are dealt with comprehensively elsewhere (Gray and Jenkins 1985; Heclo and Wildavsky 1981). Here we note simply the merging of these trends in 1970 in the government white paper entitled "The Re-organisation of Central Government" (Cmnd. 4506, 1970). This document, a brainchild of Prime Minister Edward Heath and his advisors, sought, amongst other things, to strengthen the evaluative capacity of British central government. At the cabinet level, a think tank called the Central Policy Review Staff (CPRS) was created, while a regular program of policy evaluations known as program analysis and review (PAR) was conducted in all major spending departments.

Both the CPRS and PAR had a brief heyday before falling from political and administrative grace, and both were casualties of the early years of Mrs. Thatcher's government. The CPRS has perhaps only a limited evaluative function yet one of its objectives was to persuade ministers to think strategically. Made up of civil servants, academics, and outsiders to government, part of the CPRS's task was to encourage more evaluation at cabinet level. In contrast, the PAR program was focused on departments with the objective of forcing them to analyze and evaluate their programs on a regular basis. The PAR initiative was coordinated at the center (with Treasury and CPRS involvement) but administered and conducted by the departments themselves. The intention was that regular evaluations would be fed into the public expenditure survey (PESC). From the outset this was never achieved, and within a few years the PAR program faded. As one senior administrator told a House of Commons committee some time later, "The program simply ran into the sand".

Meanwhile in British local government, a complex structural reorganization in 1974 was accompanied in many local authorities with a commitment to introduce corporate planning systems. The corporate planning "revolution," inspired by the report of the Bains Committee (Bains 1972), was based on a sharp critique of the policy management and evaluative capacity of local authorities. The latter were seen as dominated by parochial departmental views (for example, in education, housing, social services, etc.) with minimal attention paid to the way individual programs interacted with each other.

Local authorities were also criticized for devoting too little effort to both evaluating program performance and developing corporate views. In consequence, a series of changes in structure and process were suggested involving the creation of the post of chief executive, the establishment of policy-and-resources committees, and the reshaping of the decision and evaluative processes of authorities. There was no legal obligation for local government organizations to follow Bains. Some authorities were reluctant, but many embraced the new ideal wholeheartedly. Yet within ten years what remained of Bains was to be found in the rhetoric rather than the reality of local government management. Once again departmental interests dominated, policy was analyzed at a superficial level, and what passed for an evaluation of activities was rarely either comprehensive or corporate. Admittedly not all local authorities went down this path but many, if not most, did. As with PAR in central government, the corporate planning revolution faded, leaving behind some enthusiasts but also a generation of politicians and administrators suspicious, if not cynical, of instant, comprehensive managerial cures.

Looking back over the era of PPB and PAR, a senior Treasury official (and now cabinet secretary) who had lived through this period claimed that the problem with such techniques was they failed either to realize the diversity of government or to adapt to the different contexts into which they were introduced (Butler 1986). In a more specific study of the history of PAR we have argued that such innovations met a series of constraints that can be described as technical, organizational, and political (Gray and Jenkins 1982). On the technical level, information was often scarce, data bases weak, and skilled personnel unavailable. In terms of organization, departments (with rare exceptions) and the center were not well structured for evaluative activity (the absence of planning units, etc.), while both departmental and party politics provided few incentives to conduct or implement evaluations. Such schemes were seen as cosmic with few identifiable and immediate payoffs. Consequently, as soon as top-level political and department management interest decreased, the innovations (policy analysis, evaluation, etc.) waned.

Yet not all assessment should be negative. Officials connected with these programs often talk of the legacy of the processes on both the culture and rhetoric of British administration. Indeed, converts to the ideas of prioritization, analysis of policy alternatives, and the introduction of systematic evaluation, rose through the 1970s to hold senior administrative positions in British government of the 1980s. Yet many of them were also convinced that a top-down, comprehensive scheme like PPB and PAR was ill suited to the needs of departmental administration and program management. In particular, when resources were scarce a new awareness was required, not least of the cash the public sector consumed and the requirement to manage this. Consequently, the priorities of public sector management were seen to lie less with comprehensive schemes for policy analysis than with arrangements for the careful management and evaluation of resource consumption.

Policy Evaluation and Policy Analysis in a Changing Economic Climate

To focus exclusively on the micropolitical climate that existed in the 1960s and 1970s may be to neglect the influence of wider forces, not least the unstable economic world in which evaluative and budgetary control systems found themselves. For example, the demise of the PAR was as much due to its link with the volume planning of public expenditures (PESC) as it was due to its own internal weaknesses. The arguments that the PESC system rapidly went "out of control" are well charted (see, for example, Pliatzky 1984). Following the collapse of PESC, ideas on central government management focused more firmly on cash management and the control of resources than on any idea of the measurement of program output and sophisticated calculations of effectiveness.

Past analysis of budgetary innovations such as PPB in other national contexts have revealed that planning and control systems may not coexist easily. From the mid-1970s the emphasis of policy management in UK central government began to concentrate sharply on the control of resources, especially cash. It was said that too few bureaucrats viewed themselves as managers and, of these, fewer still considered themselves as responsible for the resources they consumed or the activities they oversaw. In part this was seen as a consequence both of a culture which belittled self-evaluation and of information systems which obstructed rather than facilitated it.

The view that this gave rise to both ignorance of, and indifference to, resource use was current in part of British central administration from the mid-1970s on. The advent of Mrs. Thatcher's first Conservative administration in 1979 gave it freedom to develop and flourish. The result has been a large scale program to create a new climate of management in government. It is in relation to this program that current efforts to develop schemes of policy evaluation throughout the wider structure of British government need to be understood.

Policy Evaluation in the 1980s

British Central Government

Since 1979 the main thrust of administrative reform in central-government departments has been to make such departments more self-evaluative and self-monitoring. Initially at least concepts such as accountability and control were emphasized at the expense of option analysis and evaluation. In line with such a mission, the Thatcher administration disposed of the PAR program in 1979 and wound up the CPRS in 1983. In their place appeared the Efficiency Strategy and, later, a more comprehensive program known as the Financial Management Initiative (FMI).

The Efficiency Strategy followed closely on the demise of PAR. Derek Rayner, a businessman with extensive experience of working in government, was asked to design proposals for achieving "greater efficiency" in Whitehall. The result was a program of efficiency scrutinies conducted in individual departments coordinated and directed by a small central Efficiency Unit (headed by Rayner) with direct access to the prime minister.

Broadly, the Efficiency Strategy was to have three objectives: to promote greater value for money, to remove obstacles to good management, and to encourage quick and effective implementation of feasible changes. This was to be achieved by short and sharply focused studies that examined and questioned specific departmental activities. The aim of the scrutiny program was, therefore, not only to seek savings but to advocate changes that could be implemented (Beesley 1983; Metcalfe and Richards 1984, 1987).

The strategy began on a limited scale. However, as a recent National Audit Office report noted, it has lasted with sustained access to and support from the highest levels of government (H.C. 365, 1986). On the face of things its targets may appear modest and its achievements in evaluative terms strictly limited. However, for those who control it, the impact is intended to be long term, that is, to develop not only underlying changes in behavior and attitudes but also to make self-evaluation part of regular administrative practice.

Its development attracted increasing attention, not least of a House of Commons Select Committee exploring "efficiency and effectiveness" in central government (H.C. 236, 1982). The committee spoke warmly of the strategy but believed that wider systems of program reviews and evaluations should be developed involving both the government and Parliament. In its reply to the committee the government agreed with the spirit of this point but not with the suggested method of implementation (Cmnd. 8616, 1982). Instead, it unveiled a program entitled the Financial Management Initiative (FMI). This was intended to introduce in all departments a differentiated and decentralized system in which managers at all levels had (1) clearly defined objectives and (wherever possible) the means to measure outputs and performance in relation to these objectives, (2) a defined responsibility for resource use, and (3) the support including relevant information, training, and advice necessary to exercise responsibilities effectively (Cmnd. 8616, 1982).

Initially the FMI reflected broad concerns with cost control within departments and an emphasis on achieving value for money. It also contained a strong commitment to the establishment of decentralized systems of accountable management and the development of information and monitoring systems within departmental structures. Further, and more importantly, taken together with the Efficiency Strategy, it represented a sharply contrasting approach to earlier efforts of the 1970s. In particular, if the latter were top down, policy focused, and centralized, the new era reflected bottom up, managerial, and implementable approaches that allowed departments to develop individual responses under central guidance.

As with the Efficiency Strategy, the coordination and development of the FMI was placed in the hands of a small missionary team — the Financial Management Unit (FMU). Under the team's guidance, departments were instructed to outline their plans for projected developments and priorities, to state what they were doing to manage objectives and costs, and to describe how they allocated responsibility for resources. Departments were also encouraged to develop schemes of performance indicators and output measures. By 1985 the establishment of the FMI itself was complete and its development became the responsibility of the Joint Management Unit (JMU) Treasury and Management and Personnel Office team. At the end of 1987 machinery of government changes passed responsibility to financial management group (FMG) of the Treasury.

The FMI has now been in operation for over five years. Its early progress was charted by a number of government publications (Cmnd. 9058, 1983; Cmnd. 9297, 1984) and more recently by an investigation of the National Audit Office (H.C. 588, 1986). These reports indicate a large-scale commitment of resources to the FMI and a number of discrete departmental developments. The latter include (1) the design and implementation of top management and systems, (2) the development of systems of accountable management and budgetary control at various levels of departmental hierarchies, and (3) the development of arrangements for measuring and assessing outputs and performance in relation to objectives.

There can be no doubt of the extensive effort invested in this program and the commitment of many of those who control it to change the wider culture of public service management. Nevertheless the FMI must be placed in context. It has been launched and operationalized by a government committed to controlling and reducing public expenditure and, as part of this, to reduce the size and nature of the public service itself. Taken to an extreme this may result in a fixation on inputs and rather crude and distorted interpretations of efficiency. Since the stated objectives of the FMI include promoting both efficiency and effectiveness, as well as encouraging more management discretion, there may be contradictions in both theory and practice (Gray 1986). Further, as the FMI appears to embrace an internal management control system that stresses resource use and individual management responsibility rather than the maximization of program effectiveness, a negligible role for policy evaluation might be inferred. However, this would not be the position of those who coordinate it, and certainly the current view from the FMG is that a regular system of program evaluation should be a natural development of the FMI.

Such a case has been put by a Treasury spokesman (Butler 1986), while efforts to promote departmental involvement have been initiated particularly by the JMU (Levitt 1987). For Butler, policy evaluation has become topical since, in situations where resources are static or shrinking, departmental ministers seek to protect or improve the quality of services in response to increasing public demand or external developments. This fuels the continuing battle for resources between spending departments and the center (in particular the Treasury), where there is a need to assess and compare the merits of different programs. The Treasury is too small to undertake evaluations itself: hence the necessity for departments to develop an evaluative capacity of their own.

Such thoughts have influenced both politicians and administrators responsible for guiding the FMI. In its early stages the FMI was concerned chiefly with departmental running costs and with the development of management systems at the operational level. Nevertheless, the need to extend and broaden such a program was recognized by the FMU in a report entitled "Policy Work and the FMI" (H.M. Treasury 1985). It was the political response to this that set out the subsequent demand that "all new policies or reviews of policies should include arrangements for evaluation, i.e., what is to be achieved, by when and at what cost and how that achievement is to be measured" (Levitt 1987, 49).

Acting on this brief the JMU and FMG (the successors to the FMU) have set out to encourage departments to develop policy evaluation as a regular part of policy development. It has done this through (1) establishing a guide for policy evaluation for departmental managers, (2) conducting case studies of policy evaluation in an effort to refine this guide, and (3) organizing seminars and discussions between departmental managers and those at the center to see how methods and approaches can be refined (Hogwood 1987; Levitt 1987).

As with other FMI-based activities, the emphasis is on departmental self-evaluation rather than central direction. However, within this framework the current initiatives are probably the nearest Whitehall has come since the days of PAR to encouraging regular evaluative activity. The difficulties in performing such activities are not minimized, since it is recognized that they must both differ from monitoring and grapple with the untidy problem of objectives and output measurement. It is also recognized that there is a need to develop conceptual understandings of each policy area under consideration and of the interaction of this area with the wider policy environment. Above all, the emphasis is on evaluation as a regular organized activity.

These efforts have progressed steadily over the last three years. A developmental framework is being used, with case studies and consultation employed to refine and shape evaluative models and methodology. As with the FMI, the central directives on evaluation have been cast in general terms with the implementation being the responsibility of the departments themselves (under a certain amount of central supervision and guidance). Following the initial instructions from the cabinet and Treasury concerning the need to develop an evaluative capacity in all government departments, the JMU sponsored a set of four initial case studies to illustrate the possibilities and problems of designing a coherent methodology of policy evaluation. These illustrative studies focused on such diverse areas as support programs for the microelectronics industry, the work of the UK Health and Safety Executive on new electricity safety regulations, and the effectiveness of the Alvey Program (a cross-departmental initiative to promote collaborative work within UK industry in the information technology field) (Butler 1986).

Not surprisingly, this early work indicated familiar difficulties in establishing a coherent evaluative methodology. These included problems arising from imprecise objectives, loose definitions of the scope and focus of evaluation, and inadequate organization within government departments. However, notwithstanding such difficulties, the experience of these earlier studies helped to develop a draft methodology which was used as a guiding framework in a second and larger set of evaluations involving over twenty different departments and agencies and a variety of activities and programs. On the basis of these studies, the guidelines on evaluation were further refined by central units after consultation with the departments (H.M. Treasury 1988). A major objective is to establish evaluation as an integral part of the policy management process within departments. Emphasis is being placed on the evolution of departmental capacities for organizing and conducting evaluations on a regular basis. Previous experience (for example, of PAR) has shown this can be difficult both to initiate and to sustain (Gray and Jenkins 1985; Hogwood 1987).

Parliament, Select Committees, and the National Audit Office

It would be incorrect to see developments under the aegis of the FMI as the only efforts at evaluation by Whitehall departments. Some conduct evaluative reviews on their own initiative, some hire consultants to undertake studies, while some may fund academic research from universities or research institutes (for example, in the fields of education and health). However, as Hogwood has noted, much of what is commissioned is "ad hoc and fragmentary" (1987, 237) and there is generally little in the way of controlled policy experimentation. More importantly, however, much of this work (with certain notable exceptions) remains classified or unpublished in departmental archives.

This general reluctance to open policies to public scrutiny is not confined to the British government, but the operating styles of successive British administrations, aided and abetted by the structures of the Official Secrets and Public Records Acts, make public evaluations of the policy programs of central departments problematic. In theory the role of scrutiny should be performed by Parliament, but shortage of time, resources, and the influence of party ties make it difficult for Parliament to exercise this role in an effective way. However, since 1979 there has been a strengthened system of select committees in the House of Commons, while one of the House's longest-established committees, the Public Accounts Committee (PAC), is now served by the National Audit Office (NAO) created under the Audit Act of 1983 to replace the old Exchequer and Audit Department.

Select committees of the British Parliament do not have the same weight and power as the committees of the U.S. Senate and House of Representatives (and many parliamentarians would be horrified if they had). Furthermore, they are poorly resourced in terms of research facilities, have a restricted brief (how far they can or should go into detail of policy is a matter of dispute), and produce reports that do not have to be debated or formally acted on by the government. Having said this, they can be important weapons of scrutiny (for example, after the Westland affair) and do have powers to call for witnesses and papers involved in the topic they choose to investigate. The result is a series of often substantial (although uncoordinated) reports that have potential evaluative weight. Nevertheless, the effective powers of the select committee system remain limited (Drewry 1985).

The PAC and the NAO, however, are worth special mention. The brief of the majority of the new select committees is a departmental one (for example, Agriculture, Health and Social Security). In contrast, the brief of the PAC is to provide ex post control of government spending and for this they have the services of the comptroller and auditor general (C & AG) and his staff at the NAO. Under the 1983 Act, the remit of the C & AG has been broadened from a traditional regulatory audit to include the investigation of whether departments are spending resources "economically, efficiently and effectively." As a result, there have been attempts to change the character and operation of the NAO. Staff with wider financial qualifications have been recruited, performance-related pay has been introduced, and frequent use has been made of the services of consultants.

Have such changes improved policy evaluation in the particular areas of responsibility of the PAC? Certainly there has been a great deal of activity and there can be little doubt that as report follows report, the NAO has interpreted its role more widely than before. However, it would be difficult to see its studies as evaluations. At best, they raise sharp points on the conduct of particular activities or the commitment and utilization of resources. At worst, they stand as monitoring or progress reports that fail to press home or integrate the points made. Yet this may be less the fault of the C & AG or the NAO than the consequence of the PAC's own limited powers and interests. There may be more mileage in scoring political points off the executive than expending resources producing lengthy and extensive evaluations that may only be ignored.

Local Government and the Audit Commission

The history of central-local government relations in the UK over the last eight years has been one of increasing tension and strain. Centered mostly on the vexed topic of local government finance and central controls over local authorities, this policy area has also seen the abolition of one class of local government (the Greater London and Metropolitan councils), furious debates over the provision of services, and the politicization of local councils. There have also been a number of recent proposals which would, if implemented, radically alter if not strip away many of the functions that local government currently carries out.

In all this the creation of the Audit Commission under the 1982 Local Government Finance Act might be seen as one of many attempts by the center to tighten central control over local authorities. Such an instant assessment would be misplaced, and anyone with a passing interest in policy management and policy evaluation should find the creation and development of the Audit Commission of some interest.

The Act of 1982 took the formal responsibility of appointing auditors of local authorities out of the hands of the Department of the Environment and put it into the hands of the Audit Commission. The latter was established as a "body corporate." Consequently, it does not act on behalf of the government, nor are its officers civil servants. This autonomy is important. In addition, the brief of the Audit Commission has been cast widely. Not only has it a formal audit role, but it also undertakes or promotes studies "to improve the economy, efficiency and effectiveness" of the bodies for which it had audit responsibilities. The commission has become, therefore, relatively autonomous of government, with a wide remit, and, to a great extent, free to organize and conduct itself as it see fit.

We have pointed out both the political nature of British local government and its responsibilities for the delivery of services such as housing, social services, and education. We have also noted how the problems of local government finance have been exacerbated by central attempts to control public spending. Within this climate, the Audit Commission defined part of its task as improving the management of local government, and to this end investigated services such as council housing, refuse collection, and community care. It also set out to develop data sets through which local authority performance in different service areas could be compared. The results of these activities have been a series of reports on topics varying from the management of housing and parts of the education service, to the wider areas of capital finance and revenue expenditure.

The responses to such activities have been interesting. From the side of the local authority has come both praise and criticism: praise for attempts to analyze difficult (and often unresearched) problems, and criticism for the form of the studies, the methods used in comparison, and the criteria employed to make judgments of "good practice." Further, the commission has been accused of being obsessed with cost cutting and indifferent to the complex nature of specific services, such as education and welfare, in terms of policy output and policy outcome. These are criticisms the commission denies and, in a recent annual report, it points out that "value for money is not a synonym for economy; sometimes improvements in effectiveness involve more rather than less expenditure" (Audit Commission 1986, 9).

If these debates with local authorities are of importance, so too is the fact that the commission has seen itself able to criticize government policy often in strong if not scathing terms. This applies not only to the system of local government finance that the commission's director described as "a shambles," but to policy areas such as the finance of state housing and to welfare programs such as community care. In these and other areas the blame for many difficulties has been placed either at the door of central departments or on the failure of the center to conceptualize, plan, or finance many of the policy programs that are delivered at local level.

As with the NAO, the Audit Commission has no ability to enforce its recommendations. It therefore remains an influential but toothless body. Whether it is an evaluation agency is doubtful. Nevertheless, its reports are well produced, sharply presented, and skillfully publicized. Under its first director general, John Banham, the Audit Commission adopted a high profile exploiting its quasi-independent role to draw sharp attention to the impact and effects of central and local policies. As Banham has noted, such a role is difficult to play, not least since the dividing line between management and policy "is not easy to define to the satisfaction of all the conflicting interests involved" (Audit Commission 1986, 22). The truth of this statement may be reinforced by rumors that the government, having seen what it has created, is highly unlikely to design any similar bodies in the foreseeable future.

Policy Evaluation in the UK: An Assessment of Progress

As the previous discussion should indicate, policy evaluation activities in the UK remain essentially dispersed and fragmentary in nature. Inside and outside central government there is little in the way of an established community devoted primarily to evaluation activities, nor are there coherent and established procedures for initiating, conducting, and utilizing evaluations in the policy process. This system may indeed be changing, but the status quo is not only a product of history but also a reflection of the political and administrative cultures of British government and the constraining forces that operate within it.

In central government it is for the most part the departments them-selves who initiate and conduct the evaluations and produce the reports. There are, of course, exceptions to this, and some departments may contract out evaluations to consultants or research institutes. However, if evaluative activity is contracted out it is almost inevitably carefully moni-tored, with the results being seen as departmental property. This, of course, also effects the utilization process.

There is, therefore, no separate central organization in British central government whose task is to conduct policy evaluations. Bodies such as the JMU and now the FMG play what is essentially a role of guidance. Undoubtedly, there is some mobility of personnel (that is, staff seconded from the center to departments and vice versa), but the role of the center has been, and remains, one of steering and coordination while evaluative practice is conducted within the departments. Here organization varies from department to department. Some undoubtedly have units whose roles may include specializing in analytical and evaluative activities, but many others operate on a more ad hoc basis, mobilizing teams or groups as the need arises. In all cases, the cost of evaluations falls on the depart-ments themselves and, in an era of cost consciousness, a careful eye is likely to be kept on the resources expended on evaluations, to the extent of asking what added value or benefit they actually produce.

What role do such evaluations or evaluative reports play in the policy process? A key feature of Whitehall culture is that departments serve ministers and not the collectivity of government. Evaluations that are produced are, therefore, for ministers and not the center. Similarly, evalu-ations need ministerial agreement if they are to be acted on. Central agencies can undoubtedly put pressure on outlying departments, especial-ly if they have strong backing from the prime minister (for example, the efficiency unit), but the reality of the political geography of British gov-ernment inevitably fragments the production and utilization of policy analysis and policy evaluation (Gray and Jenkins 1982, 1985).

A further consequence of the way government operates is that evalua-tions are likely to remain in the private world of government rather than to be placed in the public domain. Undoubtedly recent years have seen attempts to relax this condition, including efforts by the Efficiency Unit and the Joint Management Unit to give a public profile to these activities (see the subsection on British Central Government in this chapter). As a result, work on information systems and some of the recent case studies on policy evaluation have been made publicly available. Nevertheless, as the literature on policy evaluation and bureaucratic politics indicates, there is a consistent tension between the ideology of evaluation and the ideology of politics, especially where political actors see information as a resource to advance political, personal, or organizational interests and goals. The consequences of this for British central government is that the case for comprehensive policy evaluation may still have to be won, and, even if won, larger questions of organization and utilization will remain.

This concluding discussion so far has deliberately not referred to external evaluations such as those by parliamentary select committees or the National Audit Office. It has also not touched on the question of whether much of evaluation as practiced is *policy evaluation* in any rigorous sense of the term or some extension of audit and monitoring activities. We will now deal with these in turn.

Looking broadly at evaluative activities in the UK there would seem to be an *inverse* relationship between the scope of evaluations conducted and the proximity of evaluators to departmental activities, coupled with a *direct* relationship between the political legitimacy of evaluations and the proximity of evaluators to the activities studied. This is also overlaid by a paradox: namely that the resources available for evaluations (personnel, knowledge, developing information systems) are undoubtedly available in central administration while external agencies remain at a disadvantage in mobilizing themselves for evaluation work. The consequences of such factors for parliamentary scrutiny is that the studies conducted are often limited, uncoordinated, and poorly utilized, with little enthusiasm amongst most politicians to improve this situation. In the UK (perhaps in contrast to the United States) there are few political points to be gained for scrutinizing the executive's activities, and little payoff in investing time to develop expertise in the scrutiny area. Indeed, one may harm rather than help a political career by moving down this road. In such a climate evaluation is unlikely to flourish and there is little prospect of a strong parliamentary case being made (or won) for more resources to be devoted to it.

Nevertheless, it can be argued that in times of shrinking resources and a changing political climate (especially one that emphasizes value for money and wishes to question the existence of many government activities previously taken for granted) there *have* been positive developments. Furthermore, it could be claimed that recent activities reflect a new realism that can be contrasted with the misplaced ambition of the 1960s and early 1970s (PAR, CPRS, etc.). The foundation of such activities has been the installation of financial discipline and management in government. Such moves have sought not only to take into account cultural differences in the UK public sector, but also to change this culture so that governmental organizations conduct themselves according to the tenets of economy, efficiency, and effectiveness.

This account may be essentially true. However, to accept it at face value neglects the paradox that economy, efficiency, and effectiveness may not coexist easily and that attempts to change the administrative culture of government may be of little (or limited) value unless the political culture can change as well. It was a set of political constraints that hindered earlier initiatives (e.g., PAR). Current attempts to increase evaluative activities may remain limited unless political actors (and the organizations they are accountable for) perceive political incentives in such moves. So far there has been perhaps more political lip service to evaluation than any commitment to develop it in a rigorous fashion. As a consequence, present internal initiatives to extend evaluation, however worthy, may find themselves constrained by the political and organizational context of UK government.

References

The Audit Commission. 1986. *Report and accounts 1986*. HMSO.

Bains, M. ed. 1972. *The new local authorities: Management and structure.* HMSO.

Beesley, I. 1983. "The Rayner scrutinies." ch. 4 in A. G. Gray and W. I. Jenkins, eds. *Policy analysis and evaluation in British government.* Royal Institute of Public Administration.

Butler, R. 1986. "Programme evaluation: A central perspective." pp. 21–30 in *Policy management and policy assessment: Developments in central government.* London/New York: Royal Institute of Public Administration/Peat Marwick.

Cmnd. 4506. 1970. *The reorganisation of central government*. HMSO.

Cmnd. 8616. 1982. *Efficiency and effectiveness in the civil service.* HMSO.

Cmnd. 9058. 1983. *Financial management in government departments.* HMSO.

Cmnd. 9297. 1984. *Progress in financial management in government departments.* HMSO.

Drewry, G., ed. 1985. *The new select committees.* Oxford, U.K.: Oxford University Press.

Gray, A. G. 1986. "Policy management and policy assessment: The background." pp. 11–20 in *Policy management and policy assessment: Developments in central government.* London/New York: Royal Institute of Public Administration. Peat Marwick.

Gray, A. G., and W. I. Jenkins. 1982. "Policy analysis in British central government: The experience of PAR." *Public Administration* 60:429–50.

———. 1985. *Administrative politics in British government.* London: Harvester.

———. 1987. "Government and public administration in 1986." *Parliamentary Affairs* 40(3):299–318.

H.C. 236. 1982. *Treasury and civil service committee, efficiency, and effectiveness in the civil service.* HMSO.

H.C. 365. 1986. *39th Report from the Committee of Public Accounts. The Rayner scrutiny programmes, 1979 to 1983.* HMSO.

H.C. 588. 1986. The National Audit Office. *Report by the comptroller and auditor general. The financial management initiative.* HMSO.

H.M. Treasury. 1985. Financial Management Unit. "Policy work and the FMI."

H.M. Treasury. 1988. *Policy evaluation: A guide for managers*. HMSO.

Heclo, H., and A. Wildavsky. 1981. *The private government of public money*. 2nd ed. Macmillan.

Hennessy, P. 1986. *Cabinet*. Basil Blackwell.

Hogwood, B. 1987. *From crisis to complacency: Shaping public policy in Britain*. Oxford University Press.

Levitt, M. 1987. "Central government." ch. 3 in P. Jackson and F. Terry, eds. *Public domain: The public sector yearbook, 1987*. Public Finance Foundation.

MacGregor, J. 1987. "Measuring performance in the public services: A progress review." Paper presented to Public Finance Foundation Seminar, May 1987.

Metcalfe, L., and S. Richards. 1984. "Raynerism and efficiency in government." Ch. 10 in A. Hopwood and C. Tompkins, eds. *Issues in public sector accounting*. Philip Allan.

————. 1987. *Improving public management*. Sage.

Pliatzky, L. 1984. *Getting and spending*. 2nd ed. Basil Blackwell.

Wass, D. 1983. "United thoughts and counsels." *The Listener* 24 November, 19–21.

4

The Organization and Function of Evaluation in the United States: A Federal Overview

Ray C. Rist

Introduction

The federal budget of the United States now approaches $1,000,000,000,000 each year. While significant portions of that trillion-dollar sum are used to finance the national debt, provide social security payments to the elderly, and sustain the national defense, still more than four hundred billion dollars are spent each year on nondefense matters. How effectively those funds are used is of vital concern to the Congress, the administration, and the American public.

Policy evaluation can address this concern by tracking the use (and abuse) of those funds to learn what programs are actually in place, what services those programs are actually providing, who is making use of the programs and services, how efficiently and effectively the programs are being managed, and what the trade-offs are among different strategies to achieve policy goals.

What follows in this paper is a brief overview of the policy evaluation efforts in the United States. The paper will focus on the functions and conditions in both the executive and legislative branches of the national government. This federal-level-only perspective means that the significant efforts now under way to use policy evaluation at the state and local levels will not be addressed here.

It goes almost without saying that such a brief description as provided here will do some considerable injustice to the variations and nuances in the way the policy evaluation function is carried out among different executive-branch departments (for example, the Department of Labor does not conduct its work or organize its functions in a fashion identical to that found in the Department of Health and Human Services). Likewise, the 535 House and Senate members or the approximately 250 committees and subcommittees of the U.S. Congress do not all use policy evaluation, let alone use it in similar ways. Consequently, this paper must be viewed as a rough and therefore somewhat imprecise sketch of federal-level efforts.

The Historical Context

Although some have said the foundation for policy and evaluation research in the United States was laid back in the 1920s or earlier (Wollman 1984, 104, 118), it is more relevant to suggest that the super-structure was begun in the 1960s, particularly as a result of the massive initiatives supported under the banner of the War on Poverty by presidents Kennedy and Johnson. Policy evaluation has, by all measures, developed quite remarkably in these past nearly thirty years. The development represents the melding and maturing of two streams of intellectual inquiry during this time (Chelimsky 1985, 2). First came efforts by government managers to get control of their programs and resources via a new rationalization of the process—especially that represented by the economic management paradigm of planning, programming, and budgeting systems (PPBS). Here a variety of quantitative methods were brought to bear to rationalize the resource-allocation process. Thus the growth of cost-benefit analysis, forecasting methods, etc., all of which were aimed at projecting future outcomes of program efforts, based on the presumed linkages of inputs to outputs.

The second intellectual current that flowed into the development of policy and program evaluation during this period was that of applied social science, particularly the strategies of survey research and large-scale statistical analysis. Going all the way back to studies conducted during and after World War II, survey research became an important if not preeminent tool for social scientists attempting to understand the perceptions, attitudes, experiences, and aspirations of large segments of the population. Indeed, one strand of this work has led to public-opinion polling, which has grown so sophisticated that a sample of just more than fifteen hundred persons can be generalizable to the entire U.S. population of approximately 250 million.

Summarizing the convergence of these two strands of inquiry, Chelimsky notes:

Little by little, over time, the two paths of evaluative inquiry have become less distinct and today it is not uncommon to find a mixture of techniques from both streams used together in a single study. The yield has thus been an increasingly rich repertoire of methods for use in answering different types of questions about policies and programs. (1985, 3)

It is interesting to note that the movement of such techniques into the public sectors did not occur concurrently across government. PPBS came first into the Defense Department under Robert MacNamara in the early 1960s. Shortly thereafter, President Johnson ordered its implementation in all executive-branch agencies. Yet by 1970, its fall from grace was so dramatic that it was largely abandoned. This decline did not occur because government managers had any less desire to control their resource allocation procedures or to link these allocations to performance and program outcomes. It happened because the measures needed to justify such an approach simply did not exist. In fact, how to measure inputs was no more clear than how to measure outputs. Consequently, the assumptions were frequently far off target and the end results of the allocation process were woefully inadequate.

While fascination with the hyperrationalization offered by economic models has waned considerably, the broader concern with policy evaluation has diffused into other parts of the federal government, and policy evaluation is now seen as a necessary tool for good management.

Perhaps the ultimate legitimation of program and policy evaluation as an important tool for policymakers came in 1979 when the Office of Management and Budget (OMB) (whose director reports directly to the president) issued Circular No. A-117, entitled "Management Improvement and the Use of Evaluation in the Executive Branch." This circular, which constituted formal policy throughout the executive branch, stated explicitly:

All agencies of the Executive Branch of the Federal Government will assess the effectiveness of their programs and the efficiency with which they are conducted and seek improvement on a continuing basis so that Federal management will reflect the most progressive practices of both public and business management and result in service to the public. (OMB 1979, 1)

The end result has been an impressive array of methods, approaches, and analytic frames available to policy analysts. This is all to the good, since more ways now exist to answer the questions of policymakers. In addition, there is more understanding of just what each approach can bring, in the way of strengths and weaknesses, to that answer.

The U.S. Congress offers a second example of the different time frames by which policy and program evaluation have come into the decision-making process of the federal government. During the 1960s, the executive branch was developing its interest in and applications of PPBS, as well as beginning to fund large-scale, retrospective evaluation studies using the methods of applied social science. Such large-scale studies were undertaken in education, health, criminal justice, and housing. The Congress had no choice but to rely, in the absence of its own evaluation capability, upon the findings and reports of the executive branch. Not wanting to rely exclusively upon executive-branch material as the basis for oversight, authorization, and appropriation responsibilities, the Congress turned more and more to the U.S. General Accounting Office (GAO). This watch-dog agency provided independent assessments of the effects of these large investments in social programs.

Several commentators on the GAO have cited the Prouty Amendment to the Economic Opportunity Act of 1967, which required the GAO to assess the effectiveness of the "Great Society" poverty programs, as the turning point in congressional expectations and demands for new types of information and analysis (Mosher 1984; Wisler 1986; Rist 1987). By 1969, the GAO had produced almost fifty reports on the poverty programs. During the next ten years, the GAO gradually expanded its work in the area of program evaluation. By 1980, congressional demand was such that the GAO created an Institute for Program Evaluation which was to be staffed by applied social scientists who would work on evaluation questions across all activities of government. That group, now renamed the Program Evaluation and Methodology Division, has approximately eighty professional staff members.

Summarizing the overall mix of work in the GAO as of 1980, Mosher has written:

> Financial auditing, which with legal work had been the bread and butter of its first quarter century, comprised only 7 percent of its total workload in 1980. Management studies in the interest of economy and efficiency narrowly defined, as developed after World War II, dropped to about 29 percent. Evaluations of ongoing programs, together with cost-benefit analyses of alternative approaches to problems for the future, comprised just about one-half, and the balance, about 14 percent, was made up of special studies of one kind or another—of methodology, techniques, surveys of needs for internal planning, and so forth. (1984, 145–46)

Two summary points from Mosher's comments can be drawn. First, the same two strands of policy evaluation discussed earlier—applied social science and economic decision making—found their way into the work of the GAO and the information it supplied to Congress. Second, Congress has come to rely on these forms of data analysis for its own work, much as has the executive branch. Consequently, while the institutionalization of policy evaluation moved at a somewhat different pace in the executive and legislative branches, they both arrived at about the same place by 1980. That they have changed in the years since and are now divergent in their orientations is a theme to be developed in the latter pages of this paper.

Evaluation Activities in the Executive Branch: A Comparative Perspective

If the high-water mark of program evaluation activities and support in the executive branch was achieved in 1979 with the issuance of OMB Circular A-117, the decline under the years of the Reagan administration has been unmistakable.[1] In tracking the changes in the executive branch between 1980 and 1984, the GAO reported to Congress considerable data on the first term of Ronald Reagan (GAO 1987). What follows is a summary of the key findings of that report.

Number of Evaluation Units in Nondefense Departments and Independent Agencies

One important way of assessing how much evaluation activity is under way at the federal level is simply to count how many different units are conducting program and policy evaluations. Table 4.1 provides the total number of such units for 1980 and 1984 (GAO 1987, 59).

Number of Professional Evaluation Staff

Just as the number of nondefense units conducting evaluations has decreased, so also has the number of professional staff. In 1980, 1,507 persons were spread across the 206 units, while in 1984 the numbers were down to 1,179, a 22 percent decrease. The figure takes on added significance when one compares it to the fact that the overall federal civilian workforce went down only 6 percent in the same period (GAO 1987, 24).

Fiscal Resources

The GAO report summarizes the fiscal resource allocation changes as follows:

With regard to fiscal resources, OMB figures show an increase of 4 percent (roughly $17 billion in 1980-constant dollars) in total budget outlays (exclud-

TABLE 4.1
Number of Evaluation Units in Nondefense Departments and Independent
Agencies, 1980 and 1984

	Year		Percent Change
	1980	1984	
Department			
Agriculture	22	18	−18
Commerce	8	0	−100
Education	5	4	−20
Energy	5	4	−20
Health and Human Services	42	32	−24
Housing and Urban Development	6	3	−50
Interior	16	10	−38
Justice	19	7	−63
Labor	9	6	−33
State	1	1	0
Transportation	11	4	−64
Treasury	11	8	−27
Subtotal: departments	155	97	−37
Agency			
General Services Administration	15	13	−13
All other agencies	36	31	−14
Subtotal: Agencies	51	44	−14
Total	206	141	−32

Source: United States General Accounting office (GAO), 1987.

ing net interest) between 1980 and 1984 for the non-defense departments and selected agencies. Outlays for evaluation activities within these same departments and agencies declined from $177.4 million in 1980 to $110.9 million in 1984 (in 1980-constant dollars). Thus, while the overall budget in the non-defense cabinet departments and independent agencies increased by 4 percent, outlays for evaluation activities decreased by 37 percent. (1987, 24)

The sources for these funds to support evaluation activities came from several key sources. These include specific studies mandated by and paid for by Congress, termed "legislative set-asides," the internal budgets of the departments and agencies, or funds that are transferred from one part of the government to another in order to have a special study conducted. Table 4.2 provides information on the sources of funding for evaluations in the nondefense departments and the independent agencies (GAO 1987, 31).

Sources of Requests for Evaluations

In surveying the executive-branch departments and independent agencies as to who initials the policy evaluations that are conducted in their respective units, responses were provided in six categories. Taking only those units that reported in both 1980 and 1984, the profile for 1984 indicates that the majority of evaluations were conducted either at the request of the top officials in the organization or by administrators responsible for the operation of particular program efforts. Summing up those evaluations that would have distribution outside the individual department or agency versus those that would remain exclusively internal, the figures indicate that the external work (legislative and OMB combined) constitutes only 15 percent of the department and 5 percent of the agency evaluations. Table 4.3 provides the data for 1984 (GAO 1987, 41).

Costs and Types of Evaluation

The GAO has summarized these data as follows:

> With regard to evaluation costs, about 80 percent of all evaluations underway in 1984 cost $100,000 or less in 1984; 15 percent cost between $100,000 and $499,000; and 5 percent, above $500,000. Compared to 1980, there was a shift toward conducting more evaluations that cost under $100,000. (1987, 33)

In terms of procurements for 1984, about 26 percent of all evaluation contracts for departments were sole source, up from the 17 percent reported in 1980. Agencies decreased their proportion of sole-source awards, although in both years, few of the studies were conducted externally. Table 4.4 provides the summary data (GAO 1987, 34).

Types of Evaluation Products

The GAO summary of data in this area is as follows:

> Evaluation information can be reported in a variety of ways and in different formats. In this section we describe the number of evaluation products, types

TABLE 4.2
Sources of Evaluation Funds

Type of unit[a]	Dollars (millions)				
	1980	Percent of subtotal[b]	1984[c]	Percent of subtotal	Percent change (1980 to 1984)
Department					
Legislative set-aside	$ 46.8	40	$34.0	47	−27
Internal budget	62.5	54	37.6	52	−40
Other	7.5	6	0.7	1	−91
Subtotal	116.8	100	72.3	100	
Agency					
Legislative set-aside	.5	4	0.0	—	−100
Internal budget	10.3	91	11.1	99	8
Other	.6	5	.1	1	−83
Subtotal	11.4	100	11.2	100	
Total	128.2		83.5		−35

Source: GAO, 1987.

[a]This table includes data only from those units reporting in both 1980 and 1984.
[b]Percentages do not necessarily add to 100 due to rounding.
[c]1980-constant dollars.

TABLE 4.3
Sources of Evaluation Mandates or Requests, 1984

	Category of Unit[a]		
	In Departments	In Agencies	Total
Legislation or congressional committee	123 (11%)	29 (4%)	152 (9%)
OMB or executive order	42 (4%)	7 (1%)	49 (3%)
Top agency officials (54%)	491 (45%)	476 (69%)	967 (54%)
Program personnel (18%)	228 (21%)	94 (14%)	322 (18%)
Self-initiated (14%)	164 (15%)	77 (11%)	241 (14%)
Other	38 (3%)	6 (1%)	44 (2%)
Total evaluations	1,086	689	1,775

Source: GAO, 1987.
[a]This includes only units which reported evaluation activities in both fiscal years (FYs) 1980 and 1984.

TABLE 4.4

Costs and Types of Evaluations, 1980 and 1984

Number of Evaluations

Category of unit and type of evaluation in departments and agencies[a]	Under $100,000		$100,000–$499,999		$500,000–$999,999		$1 million or more		Total Evaluations	
	1980	1984	1980	1984	1980	1984	1980	1984	1980	1984
Internal	774	1,112	123	111	1	6	7	0	905	1,229
(percent of total)	(77)	(82)	(40)	(43)	(3)	(20)	(13)	(0)	(65)	(73)
External	224	243	184	149	36	24	48	44	492	460
(percent of total)	(22)	(18)	(60)	(57)	(97)	(80)	(87)	(100)	(35)	(27)
Contract	206	215	169	120	33	22	46	42	454	399
Competitive	158	146	142	99	30	20	40	40	370	305
Sole-source	48	69	27	21	3	2	6	2	84	94
Federal cooperative agreements and grants	18	28	15	29	3	2	2	2	38	61
Total	998	1,355	307	260	37	30	55	44	1,397	1,689
(Percent of year total)	(71)	(80)	(22)	(15)	(3)	(2)	(4)	(3)	(100)	(100)

Source: GAO, 1987.

Note: Figures include all evaluations – started, ongoing, or completed – during FY 1980 or 1984. Cost estimates include total resources expended, regardless of funding source or fiscal year in which funds were obligated. Units which had a cost accumulation system used it in calculating costs of internal evaluations. Other units estimated costs of internal evaluations using all associated costs, including salaries, personnel benefits and compensation, training, ADP, printing, travel, and indirect costs. Estimates of the costs of external evaluations include all costs associated with issuing, monitoring, and using results of the contract, grant, or cooperative agreement, as well as its direct cost.

[a]This table summarizes data provided only by units which reported evaluation activities in both 1980 and 1984.

of evaluation products, and at whose request studies were initiated. Evaluation products differ from the number of evaluation studies under way reported earlier. As the material results of studies, products may come in multiple forms; furthermore, they may be completed some time after the analysis and writing stages of a study have been finished.

Considering only those units reporting evaluation activities in fiscal years 1980 and 1984, there was a 23 percent reduction in the number of evaluation products [2,114 in 1980 versus 1,619 in 1984]. When we disaggregate these figures taking into account whether the products stem from internal or external studies, type of evaluation unit and type of product the production across subgroups is markedly different. (1987, 38)

Table 4.5 compares the types of evaluation products in detail.

Products resulting from external evaluations dropped by 64 percent, from 848 products to 304. The declines were uniform across types of products such as technical reports and oral briefings. In contrast, the aggregate number of products from internal evaluations rose slightly, from 1,266 to 1,315.

With regard to shifts in the types of products, the main change between 1980 and 1984 was a small decrease in the proportion of technical reports and a sizeable increase in the number of nontechnical reports. The increase in nontechnical reports stems primarily from internal evaluation studies conducted within agencies. Units within departments maintained their 1980 balance between technical and nontechnical products.

As table 4.5 indicates, department results were quite different from agency results. Products resulting from internal studies remained relatively stable within departments, the exception being a notable increase in oral briefings. The biggest losses were associated with external evaluations, which declined from 794 to 281. The pattern of losses was consistent across product types.

Agencies, on the other hand, reported an increase in products from internal evaluations, from 575 to 622, with much greater reliance on nontechnical reports in 1984 than in 1980 (370 versus 143, respectively, an increase of 159 percent). With the exception of letter reports to Congress, numbers of all product types decreased for external evaluations supported by the agencies.

Use and Dissemination of Evaluation Products

Executive-branch and independent agency officials were asked by the GAO how executive-branch-produced evaluations were used and disseminated. Five types of use were reported. The GAO summarized the questions and responses as follows:

TABLE 4.5
Types of Evaluation Products, 1980 and 1984

Category	Internal/external and fiscal year	Technical reports	Non-technical reports	Letter reports to Congress	Oral briefings	Policy memos or directives	Other	Total
In departments	Internal:							
	1980	234(34)	161(23)	19(3)	169(24)	93(13)	15(2)	691(100)
	1984	259(37)	123(18)	6(1)	221(32)	58(8)	26(4)	693(100)
	External:							
	1980	289(36)	165(21)	31(4)	209(26)	75(9)	25(2)	794(100)
	1984	101(35)	55(20)	15(5)	83(30)	22(8)	5(3)	281(100)
	Subtotal:							
	1980	523(35)	326(22)	50(3)	378(25)	168(11)	40(2)	1,485(100)
	1984	360(37)	178(18)	21(2)	304(31)	80(8)	31(3)	974(100)
In agencies	Internal:							
	1980	137(24)	143(25)	16(3)	211(37)	68(12)	0(0)	575(100)
	1984	82(13)	370(59)	1(0)	75(12)	92(15)	2(0)	622(100)

External:							
1980	20(37)	12(22)	0(0)	16(30)	6(11)	0(0)	54(100)
1984	13(57)	2(9)	4(17)	3(13)	0(0)	1(4)	23(100)
Subtotal:							
1980	157(25)	155(25)	16(3)	227(36)	74(12)	0(0)	629(100)
1984	95(15)	372(58)	5(1)	78(12)	92(14)	3(0)	645(100)
Total							
Internal:							
1980	371(29)	304(24)	35(3)	380(30)	161(13)	15(1)	1,266(100)
1984	341(26)	493(37)	7(1)	296(32)	150(11)	28(2)	1,315(100)
External:							
1980	309(36)	177(21)	31(4)	225(27)	81(9)	25(3)	848(100)
1984	114(37)	57(19)	19(6)	86(28)	22(7)	6(2)	304(100)
Total:							
1980	680(32)	481(23)	66(3)	605(29)	242(11)	40(2)	2,114(100)
1984	455(28)	550(34)	26(2)	382(23)	172(11)	34(2)	1,619(100)

Source: GAO, 1987.

Note: The number of products does not equal the number of evaluation studies reported in Table 4.4. Figures in parentheses are percents of yearly totals. For comparison purposes, this table presents only data from units which reported evaluation activities in both 1980 and 1984.

- acting on specific recommendations resulting from the evaluation
- taking specific actions based on information resulting from the evaluation
- using the results to reduce uncertainty or to reinforce prior thinking
- using results to increase general knowledge about the topic or to see issues differently
- using results strategically to persuade others or to support one's own position (1987, 44–45)

The evaluators reported that program personnel and top agency officials used evaluations in all these ways, but particularly to act on specific recommendations. Between 1980 and 1984, reported use increased for department and agency units, particularly by program personnel, and particularly for actions on specific recommendations. Not surprisingly, 1984 respondents generally reported somewhat closer working relationships with program managers than in 1980 and little change in working relationships with Congress or the research community.

Dissemination has never been a major evaluation expense. In 1980, about 1.9 million dollars was spent on dissemination while in 1984, about 850 thousand dollars (in 1980-constant dollars) was spent. In both years, this represented only about 1 percent of all funds. The proportionate stability, however, reflected in absolute terms a 48 percent decline in constant dollars for departments and an 82 percent decline for agencies, or about 55 percent overall.

Summary in Brief

This rather quick overview of program and policy evaluation activities in the executive branch and their changes between 1980 and 1984 can do little more than give a sense of the broad contours of current policy and practice. That the policy-evaluation effort is a sizeable one involving considerable funds, staffing, and production of reports is not in question. What the above data do indicate is that there is a current shift underway, one that marks the receding importance that policy evaluation is perceived to have on national debates. This is so, if for no other reason than because more studies are in-house, nontechnical, smaller, and aimed at the internal management and operations of the programs, not at the broader policy questions of overall program utility and impact.

Evaluation Activities in the Legislative Branch

Describing the ways policy and program evaluations are requested, conducted, and used in the legislative branch must necessarily be somewhat more tenuous than in the previous description of the executive branch. This is so for several reasons. First, the budgets of the legislative-branch support agencies are not organized so as to be able to clearly identify the amount of fiscal resources going into program and policy evaluation. With one exception (the Program Evaluation and Methodology Division of the GAO), none of the four legislative support agencies have clearly identifiable policy evaluation units. Yet, all four are intensively involved in policy analysis. Second, the legislative arena is extremely porous, in the sense that information regarding policies and programs can come to it in many different ways — from lobbyists, special interest groups, executive-branch agencies, its own support agencies, seminars attended by individual members, publications of nonprofit think tanks, and more. Owing to this diversity of sources, tracing the influences and use of policy evaluation in the decision-making context is almost impossible. Third, the information overload that characterizes any particular policy area, be that health, defense, education, criminal justice, environmental protection, and so on, means that use of that information is necessarily selective and partial. Finally, the time frame within which material can be used by Congress is frequently highly compressed. A reauthorization bill for a particular program will be debated in committee and by the two chambers for only a limited amount of time. If relevant policy and program evaluation materials do not come through that particular window of opportunity, all the technical adequacy and elegance of analysis one might have in the report become less relevant, for it is now, bluntly, of historical rather than policy relevance.

I stress these contingencies because of the differences in the use of policy evaluations between the legislative and executive branches. In the executive branch, succinctly, program managers are with their programs every day, interested in ongoing monitoring and analysis of what their programs are accomplishing, and able to fine-tune them at least yearly through budgetary and regulatory changes. The cycle of congressional attention, by contrast, is frequently one in which the program is revisited by the relevant committees in a detailed way only once in every three or five years. Congressional oversight is necessarily more broad, focused on the general direction of policies, and sporadic. Congress is not in a position to micro-manage the programs being administered by the executive branch.

Having established the necessary caveats, what follows is a brief description of how the legislative branch in the United States has created an institutional support system to provide the information it requests on any and all topics with which it must deal. This overview is best handled by brief narratives on the four congressional support agencies.

General Accounting Office

Established in 1921, the GAO is the largest of the four support agencies, having at present 5,100 staff members. The budget is just over three hundred million dollars per year. The GAO takes on studies requested of it by Congress, but it also has the authority to initiate work in areas where it believes close scrutiny would be of benefit to Congress and where government practice could be improved. The GAO is internally organized into fifteen regional offices and seven headquarters divisions. (The staff are approximately equally divided between regions and headquarters.) A key attribute and strength of the GAO is the existence of the regional offices where several thousand staff are involved in primary data collection and analysis. The work of the regional offices is done on-site — be it a military installation, nuclear power plant, Native Indian reservation, or national forest. Working in conjunction with the headquarters divisions where the central planning and prioritizing of work for the agency is undertaken, the regional offices provide a worldwide capability to gather and analyze data relevant to the needs of congressional users.

The policy analyses conducted by the GAO are both retrospective and prospective. Retrospective work focuses on evaluations and audits of existing or past programs, while the prospective work uses modeling, simulation, or time-series data to project what might be anticipated from future changes in programs or policies. Prospective work also focuses on broader national demographic trends that must be accounted for in new legislation. This mix of retrospective and prospective work cuts across all substantive areas in which the GAO does its work. However, it should be stressed that the stronger emphasis is upon the retrospective work, particularly as it addresses matters of policy implementation and accountability. The prospective work is more clearly linked to policy formulation, an area the GAO has come to address more directly only in recent years.

The GAO has approximately 1,050 studies in progress at any one time. The results of these studies are provided to Congress via a number of channels, including formal reports with recommendations, briefing reports, fact sheets, letter reports, briefings, testimony, and comments on pending legislation. Each of these means of conveying information to the relevant congressional user is intended to enhance the usefulness and timeliness of the work GAO does. This mix of dissemination strategies has evolved as a result of recognizing the diversity of ways information comes to Congress and that different strategies must be in place to meet different informational needs.

All reports produced by the GAO are in the public domain, free of charge to anyone who asks, and is available to anyone anywhere, so long as the report does not deal with a classified matter of national security and defense.

Library of Congress and the Congressional Research Service

Information is an indispensable tool for a member of Congress, especially if it is accurate, accessible, and presented in a form that is readily understood. One of the major sources of such information for Congress is the Library of Congress, established in 1800, and its research center, the Congressional Research Service (CRS), established in 1946. The emphasis here is less on its function as the national library of the United States than as a center to assist Congress in gathering information on national (and even local) issues. The nearly 850 staff members in the CRS, organized into seven research divisions, serve as a pool of reference and research expertise across all the major topics that Congress must address (Gude 1985).

The information that the CRS provides to Congress is confidential and reserved only for the use of the member and his or her staff, unless that member decides to make the information public. The material is presented in several forms — as reports, summaries of legal research and analysis, background summaries of the key issues to be addressed in congressional hearings, and material to be used in drafting speeches. The CRS also maintains an on-line computer system containing the status of current legislative proposals, background information (called Issue Briefs) on those proposals, and a collection of more than ten thousand organizations, place names, and contacts to be consulted on almost any topic.

The CRS does not collect original data for the reports it prepares, but rather serves as a center of synthesis for material that is already published. In this way, the CRS is used by Congress as a quick-response resource, in contrast to the other three support agencies where the work is typically of longer duration and may involve original data collection, consultation with national experts, and the development of extensive computer analyses. This quick-response emphasis in the CRS is but one example of the way in which it strives to make information as useful as possible to the congressional requestor. Another such strategy is that the information only goes to the person who requested the material, not to all members; and the CRS tries to make sure that when material reaches a member, it is what was requested and no more. In this way, the CRS seeks to avoid adding to the information overload. (There is a clear logic in all this, as the CRS received in 1984, for example, more than 430 thousand different requests for information from Congress.)

Office of Technology Assessment

Recognizing the increasingly pervasive and controversial role that technology was coming to play in American society, Congress created the Office of Technology Assessment (OTA) in 1972. The emphasis of this agency is specifically to provide Congress with assessments or analyses of the range of probable positive and negative consequences, social as well as physical, of policy alternatives affecting the uses of technology. The OTA's mandate reflects this emphasis on understanding the consequences of various policy options across a wide variety of technological areas, including health, defense, environment, communications and information, transportation, food, and biological applications, to name but a few.

The OTA provides assistance to Congress by

- identifying existing or probable impacts of technology or technological programs;
- ascertaining, where possible, the cause-and-effect relationships of the applications of technology;
- identifying alternative technological methods of implementing policy objectives;
- estimating and comparing the impacts of alternative methods and programs;
- identifying areas where additional research or data collection are required to provide support for future assessments (OTA 1986, 55).

Given the complexity of the issues and the time necessary for the OTA to carry out requests from Congress, it is not surprising that the yearly number of products is small. In 1986, the OTA delivered forty-four published documents to Congress. These included nineteen assessment reports, five technical memoranda, six background papers, one health-technology case study, nine special reports, and four administrative reports (OTA 1986, 58). These materials were produced by the 146 persons on staff. The OTA has produced 199 nonclassified reports since its inception, and all are available to the public. Examples of studies published in 1986 include "Status of Biomedical Research and Related Technology for Tropical Diseases," "Electronic Surveillance and Civil Liberties," "Reproductive Health Hazards in the Workplace," "Technology and Structural Unemployment: Reemploying Displaced Workers," and "Transportation of Hazardous Waste."

The OTA is guided by a bipartisan congressional board — six members from the Senate and six from the House of Representatives. Its small staff is augmented for almost every study by panels of national experts who are brought together specifically for the requested assessment. This private-sector involvement is a distinguishing characteristic of the OTA's work. Contractors and consultants are drawn from a wide variety of substantive and organizational backgrounds, including industry, universities, private research foundations, professional organizations, and public-interest groups.

Congressional Budget Office

In 1974, Congress passed an important piece of legislation that restructured how it dealt with the budget of the federal government. This act established guidelines for how appropriations are to be determined, what level of revenue needs to be collected, and whether the yearly budget would have a surplus or a deficit and the size of the same. To help implement this new process, the Congressional Budget Office (CBO) was created in this same 1974 legislation. The CBO functions as a nonpartisan organization that provides information to Congress on the budget and develops analyses of the costs of alternative policy options. The CBO makes no recommendations about various alternatives. Its principle task is to array the budgetary options and their costs (Congressional Quarterly 1982, 564).

The staff of the CBO is approximately 210 persons divided among six major departments: budget analysis, fiscal analysis, tax analysis, natural resources and commerce, human resources and community development, and national security and international affairs.

For each legislative proposal passed by a congressional committee, the CBO will provide information on the five-year projected budgetary impacts. Consequently, members of Congress will have information on the cost implications over time and are thus in a better position to assess options. The CBO provides more than a thousand such individual legislative projections each year. It also issues approximately sixty special reports yearly on topics of broad interest to Congress, for example, health care costs, trade, taxes, inflation, and defense spending. Almost all of the work produced by the CBO is available to the public, save for reasons of national security or because of specific congressional guidance not to release a report.

Summary

This brief overview of the four support agencies to the U.S. Congress indicates the broad base of policy analysis and information that is available to inform any particular policy debate. Congress has access to both prospective and retrospective analyses, budgetary options, and assessments of technological changes, both present and projected, as well as to detailed summaries of current knowlege on policy-relevant topics. The tasks confronting potential users of such information are to ensure that the request for help goes to the most appropriate agency, that the questions are appropriately framed, and that the time-sensitive nature of the information is clearly understood. If even elementary care is taken to effect a correct match between the needs of the information user and the appropriate congressional support agency, the user should be rewarded with more than adequate information and analysis to assist in the policy process. The U.S. Congress has more than six thousand staff members dedicated to the development and assessment of policy-relevant information. With a support base of that size and substantive diversity, the information flow to Congress can be more appropriately characterized as a flood than a stream. But how it is then used, of course, is material for another paper.

Note

The views expressed here are those of the author and no endorsement by the United States General Accounting Office is intended or should be inferred.

1. Circular A-117 was rescinded by order of the OMB director, David Stockman, on 7 March 1983. There is, at present, no executive-branch guidance on the use of program and policy evaluation.

References

Chelimsky, E. 1985. "Old patterns and new directions in program evaluation." Pp. 1–35 in E. Chelimsky, ed. *Program evaluation: Patterns and directions.* Washington, D.C.: American Society for Public Administration.

Congressional Quarterly. 1982. *Guide to Congress.* Washington, D.C.: Congressional Quarterly, Inc.

GAO. See United States General Accounting Office.

Gude, G. 1985. "Congressional research service: The research and information arm of Congress." *Government Information Quarterly* 2(1):5–11.

Mosher, F. 1984. *A tale of two agencies.* Baton Rouge, La.: Louisiana State University Press.

Office of Management and Budget. 1979. Circular No. A-117. "Management improvement and the use of evaluation in the executive branch." Washington, D.C.: OMB.

Office of Technology Assessment. 1986. *Annual report to the Congress.* Washington, D.C.: OTA.

Rist, R. 1987. "Social science analysis and congressional uses: The case of the

United States General Accounting Office." in M. Bulmer, ed. *Social Science Research and Government*. Cambridge, England: Cambridge University Press.

United States General Accounting Office. 1987. *Federal evaluation: Fewer units, reduced resources, different studies from 1980. (PEMD-87-9)*. Washington, D.C.: U.S. GAO.

Wisler, C. 1986. "Topics in evaluation." *GAO Review*. 20 (2).

Wollman, H. 1984. "Emergence and development of policy research in the U.S.A." Pp. 101–30 in G. Thurn, ed. *Development and present state of public policy research: Country studies in comparative perspective*. Berlin, West Germany: Wissenschaftszentrum.

III

Countries in the Second Wave of Evaluation Development

5

Evaluation in Denmark: The State of the Art

Erik Albaek and Søren Winter

Why Evaluation Came So Late to Denmark

Evaluation research is a fairly new activity in Denmark. Though it has been known for some time, albeit under different names, evaluation research is very much a phenomenon of the late 1970s and, especially, the 1980s. It is not easy to explain why Denmark has experienced so little evaluation compared to other countries. In the United States the growth of the evaluation industry was connected to the expansion of the welfare state in the 1960s and 1970s. But Denmark is one of the most developed welfare states in the world with one of the largest public sectors.

Explanations must probably be identified both on the demand and supply sides in relation to evaluation. With regard to the demand for evaluation, Denmark has alternative feedback mechanisms to inform policymakers and administrators about the implementation of public policies. Because the country is so small, such information is more easily spread than in a large country like the United States. Besides, policy making and implementation is characterized by a corporatist structure with strong sectorial networks between administrative agencies and affected interest organizations, which have some incentive to report perceived implementation problems to the government.

The demand for evaluation is probably also related to the level of conflict and power among political actors. Unlike in the American situation, a substantial part of Danish welfare-state legislation has had a rather broad consensus. Evaluation was not regarded as a necessary instrument by the supporters of new policies for persuading opponents, nor by opponents for getting ammunition for challenging the success of a particular program — as has been the role of evaluation in the United States. This may be due both to a relatively high degree of homogeneity in Danish political attitudes towards the welfare state and to a political structure which offers fewer incentives and resources for conflict. The American separation of powers and federalism, as well as the weak party discipline, tend to institutionalize conflict and to create more autonomous groups of political actors who can use evaluation as an instrument for policy making and control. For example, Congress sees it as its role to control and criticize the president and his executives — and even more so when the president and the majority in Congress belong to different parties.

In contrast, the Danish parliamentary system has a strong party discipline, which tends to prevent conflicts between government and legislature. In fact, the political parties supporting the government normally do what they can to protect the government against criticism. In such a system the number of actors demanding evaluation to control and criticize governmental performance is likely to be much smaller than in the United States, and Danish governments have not needed many evaluations in order to legitimize their policy programs. As mentioned above, the Danish welfare-state policy has had a rather broad consensus. Many major policy programs have been compromises between the government and the opposition, and even when the government was overruled, the former opposition very rarely changed the program when it became the government itself.

In addition, the Danish party discipline to some extent even spreads to local governments, which do not have the same incentives as the American ones to use evaluations as an instrument in conflicts with federal and state authorities. Besides, Denmark does not use so many nongovernmental organizations to deliver services, and there is consequently less need to control such organizations by evaluations.

The low level of conflict is reinforced by the high degree of homogeneity in Denmark, both at the national level and among local governments. The low level of conflict and the confidence in the ability of welfare-state policies to solve problems in society is not very stimulating to the demand for evaluations. Again, the corporatism in policy making and implementation may have contributed to the low level of conflict in Denmark.

Legislation also seems to have much more authority and legitimacy in Denmark than in the United States. People have generally been inclined to follow regulations and, perhaps even more, to believe that laws are actually implemented as expected in Parliament. Neither have the Danes experienced such visible failures of public-policy programs as has the United States concerning the great welfare programs.

With regard to the supply of evaluation, the number of people with social-science degrees and with knowledge of social-science and evaluation methodology was rather low in the 1960s and 1970s when this kind of research became popular in the United States. The central bureaucracy was still dominated by the legal profession, for which evaluation is a rather unfamiliar concept. Though the number of bureaucrats with a social-science degree has increased considerably since then, there is still very little systematic teaching in evaluation methods taking place at Danish universities, as we shall see later.

Structure and Size

Evaluation research is part of a broader effort to enhance the immediate usefulness of social-science research in public policy making, that is, to make social science research more "applied". In the early 1980s an investigation was conducted under the auspices of the Danish Social Science Research Council to find out how applied social-science research had developed in Denmark.

Though it covers more than evaluation research, the main results of the report may give a general impression of the way applied social-science research — evaluation research being a central part of this — has developed in Denmark, especially during the 1970s.

Broadly speaking, applied social-science research — or "sectorial" research, as it is named in Denmark due to its relevance for different sectors in Danish society — is carried out at institutions of higher education, within the public administration itself, or at so-called institutes of sectorial research. The last refers to research institutions established with the specific aim of doing research of an immediate usefulness for various policymakers. Among these institutions are the Danish Building Research Institute, established in 1947 and closely connected with the Ministry of Housing; the Danish National Institute of Social Research, established in 1958 and closely connected with the Ministries of Social Welfare and Labor; and the Local Governments' Research Institute on Public Finance and Administration, established in 1975 and closely connected with the Danish associations of local governments. None of these institutes have students. They are first and foremost geared towards the production of applied social-science research.

Formerly, little or no applied social-science research was carried out at the institutes of higher education. Most research was defined and carried out by tenured professors. During the 1970s a change took place. More and more research was financed from outside the universities, and often the sponsor would be a ministry or another public agency in need of having a specific social problem or program investigated or evaluated. Often younger, nontenured social scientists would be involved in this kind of research. There was a merging of interests between sponsors and younger social scientists: the former wanted to have research done; the latter were needed to be funded to do research, as the prospect of getting a tenured university professorship was quite hopeless.

Little has been done to evaluate the size and organization of social-science research conducted within the public administration itself. But as we shall see later, there is generally little systematic evaluation performed here. However, some evaluation is done by the Ministry of Finance, the Department of the Auditor General, and the Department for Development Aid. At sectorial research institutions and institutions of higher education, applied social-science research is known to have increased quite substantially during the 1970s. All in all, social-science research in Denmark, measured by full-time research staff, has increased by 14 percent from 1976 to 1982. This is almost all due to an increase in externally financed research, that is, research funded by sponsors outside the research institutions. Though not all externally financed research is applied or sectorial, a substantial part can be expected to be so. The report concludes that in 1982 *40 percent of all social-science research in Denmark can be defined as applied or sectorial in nature.*

However, as yet little is known about the exact nature, size, and organization of sectorial social-science research in Denmark, and it is difficult to say how much can properly be defined as evaluation research.

The Character and Development of Evaluation

Low Activity until the Late 1970s

As mentioned above, evaluation started much later in Denmark than in either the United States or in many other Western democratic nations, including Sweden and Norway. If evaluation is defined as systematic analysis of effects and performances of public policies, traditional auditing was probably the first major attempt to analyze the performance of the public sector. But until very recently, auditing only comprised examinations of whether agencies had spent more money than granted or had used the money for other purposes than appropriated. Performances, productivity, and effects of public programs were by and large ignored.

This does not mean that there was no feedback to policymakers and administrators about the way policies worked out, but generally such information was collected in a very unsystematic way through on-the-job experience, public debate, and contacts between citizens, interest organizations, and legislators.

For many decades Danish citizens have had the right to complain of the way their cases have been treated to higher administrative agencies or to independent administrative boards of appeal. But again, the complaints give no systematic feedback about the impact of laws and, even more important, the information has very rarely been collected and used in any systematic way for the purpose of reconsidering policies and their implementation. Since 1955 people may also complain of the way they have been treated to the ombudsman. Although his work is dominated by handling single cases, it does happen that he also pays attention to more general principles and asks the administration to change the way a law is implemented.

When the government felt that existing laws did not function in a satisfactory way, the normal procedure has been either for the administration to make a draft for a new bill or to revise the previous law, or for a royal commission to be established to consider the need for changing the rules. Typically, the affected parts of the public sector, interest organizations, experts, and sometimes politicians are represented in these commissions.

As a starting point for proposals of change, the reports of such commissions often make some kind of judgement about the effects and implementation of the existing law. But until the 1980s there were only very few cases where these judgements were based on evaluation research. Rather, they were based on the daily experience of the involved organizational actors. If any kind of scientific analysis was used, it was typically statistical data from the Bureau of Statistics or, in a few cases, research describing the problematic conditions.

Until the end of the 1970s very little systematic policy evaluation took place in Denmark. Within some professional disciplines, such as medicine and education, evaluation and experimentation took place earlier, but these were part of the development of the professional and scientific disciplines rather than evaluation of public policies. However, a few evaluations did take place. For example, the Danish National Institute of Social Research made about one evaluation study, on average, per year from 1960 to 1978. And this institute was the leading research institute for making applied social-science research in that period.

While very little evaluation took place in Denmark until the late 1970s, since then the number of evaluations has increased, both within the government itself and within research institutes, and recently also within consulting firms.

Increasing Internal State Evaluation

Generally, it is our impression that very little evaluation is performed by the ministries and local governments themselves. Important exceptions are the Ministry of Finance and the DANIDA, the department for aid to the Third World. Within the former ministry, the Department of the Budget has been inspired by the American planning, programming, and budgeting system (PBBS) to include some information about performance and productivity in the budget, and in recent years the department has published some small-scale policy evaluations of the productivity or cost-effectiveness type about various public-sector functions. Productivity analyses will probably be emphasized more by the department in the future.

Also, the Ministry of the Interior has become more interested in productivity studies. It now publishes an annual report about key indicators for various local government functions. This allows for rough comparisons of productivity among local government units. The ministry has also started comparing the productivity of the Danish hospitals.

Another department in the Ministry of Finance, the Department of Administration and Reorganization, has regularly evaluated various policy areas since 1973/74, for example, the use of resources in civil defense, the system of appeal within the social-welfare system, and the functioning of the unemployment-insurance administration. Typically, one or two studies per year are made, and the perspective of the studies is usually an analysis of options for increasing efficiency by reducing costs, like the Dutch Reconsiderations Procedure. Its methods are not very sophisticated or systematic. Various kinds of organizational analyses dominate the studies. The impact of the studies, the majority of which are published, has not been profound. The department is likely to give a lower priority to that kind of evaluation in the future.

Internationally, aid to the Third World has been one of the popular targets for evaluation studies, and the Danish DANIDA also has a special section and a network of external consultants to evaluate almost all aid projects. Generally, the evaluation methods applied are weak, mainly consisting of field visits lasting from one to a few weeks. The studies are not particularly critical, and they are not published.

The auditor general has recently begun to supplement the traditional audit methods, as mentioned above, with analyses relating costs with performance and effect, primarily inspired by the methodological development of performance auditing which has taken place in the United States, Canada, and Sweden. Productivity studies and comparisons are becoming more important, and a few simple evaluation studies focusing on effects and costs have been made. However, the traditional audit methods still dominate. Because of the auditor general's independence from the government, some of its analyses have been able to stimulate a debate in the public and in Parliament.

Increasing Evaluation by Research Institutes

While some public agencies have started to do evaluations of a more systematic character (though their design and methods are still quite simple and not very scientific), research institutes have also become much more involved in evaluation research since the late 1970s. To illustrate this point, the Social Research Institute has tripled its evaluation studies since 1979 and now makes about three studies per year. In the same period, the Local Governments' Research Institute on Public Finance and Administration has made about five evaluation and productivity studies per year.

Most evaluation studies have probably been commissioned by social welfare, labor, and education authorities dominated by central authorities in government and the associations of municipalities and counties, though single local governments have also funded evaluations.

The Ministry of Social Welfare only engaged in a few evaluations in the period from 1960 to 1979, mostly performed by the Social Research Institute. A major evaluation study of the functioning of the entire social-welfare system was, however, undertaken in 1970 as a part of the decision-making basis for a reform of the total welfare system. Also an evaluation project costing approximately 1.5 million dollars was undertaken to evaluate the reform in the early 1980s.

The recent growth in evaluation of social-welfare policies seems to be related to increasing activities of local experimentation within the sector. A general local government experiment is going on in which a number of local governments are allowed to change existing rules and practices. Experimentation has also become popular within sectors other than social welfare, such as health, education, employment, and telecommunications. Although there is still no general inclination to evaluate such experiments, some experiments are evaluated after all, and thus experimentation seems to stimulate evaluation.

The growing unemployment since the oil crisis in 1973/74 has been met by many different measures, with rather uncertain effects. The Ministries of Labor and Education are responsible for these measures, and have initiated and funded many social-science studies of the unemployment problem and evaluations of unemployment programs. From 1980 to 1983 about 1 million dollars were spent annually on applied unemployment research.

Both the growth of experimentation and evaluation—whether related to experiments or to existing programs—follow from a general conception of policy that is much more critical towards the effects of the existing welfare policies and skeptical about growing expenditures in a time of scarce resources. This attitude has stimulated reconsideration of existing welfare policies and experimentation. However, the criticism of existing welfare policies and the desire for experiments has been particularly promoted after the conservative four-party government took over in 1982. This government is not particularly fond of outcome evaluations, but evaluation sometimes becomes a political condition for starting an experiment, and so experimentation furthers evaluation.

After the advent of the conservative government, the political climate seems to be characterized by more conflict than before, and evaluation has begun to become an instrument in the fights between supporters and opponents of policies. Though the government is very reluctant about outcome evaluation, there seems to be a growing interest within the government, and particularly within the Ministry of Finance, in measuring performance in terms of productivity. It is important to note, however, that this implies an interest, not in effectiveness, but in efficiency and expenditures as an attempt to decrease or stop the growth of the public sector. As such, the productivity interest is a part of a counterreform movement very different from the reform movement that stimulated the growth of the evaluation industry in the United States in the 1960s and 1970s.

Methods for Evaluating Policy Output

The late development of evaluation research in Denmark has been accompanied by a rather modest development of evaluation methods. A number of different methods have been used, from the administrative evaluations by the Department of Administration and Reorganization and DANIDA, which rarely apply social-science methods, through rather summative studies focusing mainly on goal fulfillment and relating success to the individual characteristics of the clients of the investigated program, to more methodologically advanced studies. Process-oriented evaluations have been popular, but only a few studies have used experimental or quasi-experimental evaluation methods. Generally speaking, most studies have been methodologically weak. With a few exceptions, the administrative structure and process have been regarded as a black box or simply ignored.

The discipline of evaluation has been developed very little in Denmark. There is no university institute which has specialized in teaching evaluation. There is no professorship in evaluation; only a few university programs offer short courses in evaluation, and those only on an irregular basis. There are only a couple of small textbooks in Danish about the subject, and teaching is mainly based on American literature. There is no Danish journal for evaluation studies or policy studies, and there is very little contact between scholars who do evaluation analysis, though a few workshops have been arranged during recent years. Evaluation scholars have typically restricted their interest in evaluation to the very project in which they are engaged, and only a couple of scholars have been interested in generalizing about methodology or results.

The weak evaluation methods, the limited scope, and the lack of cumulation have also been aggravated by the fact that many evaluators started their careers in evaluation studies with only a temporary job. Therefore they had too little experience and knowledge about evaluation when they started and time limits too tight to allow them to read the literature, and they tended to leave the evaluation business after completing the job.

While most evaluation studies have focused on effect and process evaluation, Denmark has recently experienced other kinds of evaluation concerning policy output. During the 1980s productivity analyses have become more popular. It was almost a taboo in the early 1980s, when only a few scholars from research institutes dared to perform and publish productivity studies.

Implementation research is related to evaluation studies — particularly formative, process-oriented evaluation research — but generally the former focuses more on the role of the administration and the implementation process in affecting the impact of policy programs. Also, implementation researchers are more interested in generalizing and building theory about the way policies are implemented than are evaluation researchers. Implementation research started to bloom in the United States in the middle of the 1970s, but did not reach Denmark until the early 1980s. Still, however, only a couple of scholars do implementation research.

Finally, the American interest for the (non-)utilization of evaluation results in policy-making processes has also spread to a few Danish scholars.

Because of the growing interest — both from the public agencies and from university students and applied-research institutes — in evaluation, productivity, implementation, and the utilization issue, the discipline of output evaluation in a broad sense is likely to grow and mature in Denmark in coming years.

6

Policy Evaluation in the Netherlands: Institutional Context and State of Affairs

M. L. Bemelmans-Videc, R. Elte, and E. Koolhaas

Introduction

The purpose of this paper is to offer a survey of the main actors involved in and institutional arrangements created for the evaluation of (central-) government policy/programs in the Netherlands. In picturing the institutional context, we shall also give an indication of the state of affairs in policy evaluation practice.

The history of the introduction of policy-analytical methods and techniques is the subject of our first section, where we start from a short review of the traditional actors in administrative monitoring, control, and evaluation. In the second section we shall give a survey of the actors involved in policy evaluation in its more modern sense as well as qualifying remarks regarding initiation, methods, and criteria of policy evaluation. The so-called Reconsiderations Procedure (initiated in 1981) will figure as a main example of the impact of policy evaluation on political decision making.

We suggest the following definitions of the key concepts used in this paper.

Policy evaluation is part of policy analysis and includes two elements: prospective (ex ante) and retrospective (ex post) evaluation.

Policy analysis is understood in the applied, prescriptive, and multidisciplinary sense and is (therefore) meant to improve the quality of policies and administrative processes.

Evaluation implies judgement in the light of certain criteria. In political and administrative practice, these criteria may be nebulous, politically streamlined, or at least not made explicit. The attempt to realize more rational policies and administrative processes explicitly requires clarification of evaluation criteria. The working group agreed to concentrate on *retrospective policy evaluation* (evaluation ex post). We shall discern

- evaluation of the effects of a policy program for the desired condition of the societal process (for example the number of unemployed), using the term "program effect evaluation." Dominant evaluation criteria are effectiveness, efficiency, and timeliness.
- evaluation of the administrative process, concentrating on the evaluation of the actual practice of implementation. In most democratic countries, administrative practice is usually judged by (at least) the evaluation criteria of effectiveness, efficiency, democracy, and lawfulness. (One could, of course, think of more evaluation criteria: see, for example, Arvidsson 1986, 637.)

The Introduction of Policy-Analytical
Methods in the Administrative Process

Among the actors involved in policy evaluation are a number of institutes which — by law and tradition — execute a controlling function of some sort: Parliament, the General Accounting Chamber *(Algemene Rekenkamer)*, and the Ministry of Finance (in particular the Inspectorate of Finance), as well as accountancy units within the individual departments, Inspectorates on various fields of government intervention, and courts of justice (insofar as they are involved in evaluating administrative practice).

After World War II, a role of increasing importance was played by planning bureaus — especially the economic Central Planning Bureau and by advisory organs.

The establishment of a unit, with the Ministry of Finance, formally commissioned to promote policy analysis and evaluation, was to take place in the early 1970s.

Parliament *(de Staten-Generaal)* has two chambers *(Kamers)*, the First Chamber (or Senate, elected by the provincial chambers), and the Second Chamber, the representative organ in its strict sense.

The most important instrument available to the Second Chamber in its controlling function is the "budget right," implying the ex ante verification and approbation of the budget and the policy programs involved, and the ex post review, government being held accountable to Parliament.

The task of the supreme audit institution, the General Accounting Chamber *(Algemene Rekenkamer)* is directly linked to the Parliament's budget right: it should meet Parliament's information needs with regard to government budget expenditures (verification and evaluation ex post).

The General Accounting Chamber (GAC) is one of the high Colleges of State, a research institute with a constitutionally based task and with an independent position (guaranteed by law) in both its relation to government and to Parliament. Both chambers of Parliament may request the GAC to start certain researches; however, it is up to the GAC to decide whether to accept those requests.

The obligatory task of the GAC is the verification of the lawfulness of the public accounts, preceding their formal approval. Its studies may also comprise the review of policy/programs and of organizations in terms of efficiency.

The GAC informs Parliament, executive offices, the media, and the general public via annual reports and via ad hoc reports on the results of certain research projects which usually concern more elaborate studies of a policy field. The GAC has recently given more and more attention to evaluating the efficiency (and, to a lesser degree, effectiveness) of administrative practices and policy/programs. Next to comments on budgetary affairs, it pays attention to questions of management and organization, for example, the matter of administrative automation with government. This reorientation in its activities is part of a general call—to a great part, GAC-induced—for closer inspection of government management.

Until the recent past, the use made of the GAC reports by Parliament has been judged as insufficient: Parliament ought to be more interested in the execution of its own and government's decisions (Tweede Kamer der S. G. 1985–86, 19336, 1/2).

The GAC has recently pointed out that the ministerial departments effect changes in the government budget for many billions of Dutch guilders a year, without Parliament formally approving of these expenditures. The GAC stipulated that this development meant a serious depreciation of Parliament's budget right.

Parliament, especially the Second Chamber, is apparently more interested in budget control ex ante than ex post, more in policy initiation than in policy implementation. Of course, there are political reasons for this lack of interest: more political credit may be won by designing a new policy and by having Parliament accept a new law than by evaluating existing policy/programs (with possible negative outcomes). Lawfulness of expenditures (the dominant evaluation criterion in the GAC reports so far) hardly appeals to voters' imagination. With an increasing attention to efficiency, the GAC reports may gain in political momentum (van Braband 1987, 81–89).

Recently, a number of GAC reports on money-consuming projects like the *Oosterscheldedam* (in the province of Zeeland) or, for example, a report on the nation's health care have occupied a great deal of the Second Chamber's time and attention.

These developments and a number of scandals related to government spending[1] have induced a change in the political climate and a revival in the interest in government's administrative organization and internal control.[2] Both the administrative organization and internal control have been criticized as defective (caused by the sharp increase in government expenditures, the complexity of laws and rules, and by the process of automation).

From Parliament came the initiative to start a fact-finding procedure to improve the information available to Parliament on policy implementation and expenditures relating to policy implementation.[3] This fact-finding procedure is part of the preparation of the discussion of the budget in the Second Chamber.

The permanent committees of the Second Chamber (on the various policy fields) will scrutinize selected parts of the budget and see to it that they are optimally informed about facts and figures by the departments involved, by the departmental accountancy agencies, by the GAC and—if relevant—via the reports of the Reconsiderations Procedure (see the next section).

These committees also regard it as their responsibility to form an opinion on the administrative organization, the financial auditing activities of the departmental accountancy agencies, and the management of the budgetary process in the relevant fields. To conduct these researches, the Second Chamber has been granted a small staff of experts and may also involve external expertise.

So far, comments from various quarters indicate that the procedure is a success.

The tasks of the accounting agencies of the individual ministerial departments and of the Central Accounting Agency of the Ministry of Finance include financial verification of the accounts (financial auditing). Insofar as they include checks on effectiveness and efficiency, one may label their work as management auditing. Recent legislation[4] has caused these agencies to see it as their tasks to report on the shortcomings of the administrative organization and related measures of internal control and to advise on necessary improvements.

Preventive supervision of the budget is in the hands of the Ministry of Finance (in particular the Inspectorate of Finance, a subdivision of the Directorate General of the Budget).

The Inspectorates *(Inspecties)* are the classical institutes with monitoring and controlling functions, including, for example, the inspectorates of Health, of Education, of Taxes, etc. They are de-concentrated state offices that have an "eye-and-ear" function in the respective policy fields, sometimes combined with an executive function (for example, the Inspectorate of Taxes). Their evaluatory tasks are as a rule limited to the evaluation of administrative practices; program effect evaluation is a much rarer phenomenon (Commissie Hoodstructuur Ryhsdienst 1980, 222), although some of the inspectorates are redefining their tasks in that direction.

Relevant process data are, of course, also produced by the departmental units of the government organization itself. As far as the use made of these data is covered in our definition of policy evaluation, we shall say more about it in the next section.

Some of the methods nowadays labeled as "policy analysis" have been practiced since the 1930s in the Netherlands, be it on a small scale and in a limited field of (economic) policy. In the 1930s, Jan Tinbergen c.s. was to lay the foundations of "the engineering science of econometrics" (as Tinbergen called it) while working with the Central Bureau of Statistics (CBS); the functions attributed to this new branch of economic science were identical to those attributed to policy analysis these days. Times of crisis has created a new conception of the government role: one increasingly regulating social and economic life. This new conception also created a new function for economic science: to provide social-economic policy with a scientific rationale. As a consequence, discussions regarding economic-political issues would be transferred from ideological controversies to "rational" tests of alternative policy measures. The desired empirical verification and foundation of economic theory required an adequate data base and statistical-mathematical analysis. In the Netherlands, the process of the emancipation of economics and of statistics had been closely linked. Tinbergen entered the service of the CBS in 1927 to work with the section in charge of the development of business-cycle research. Pragmatic intentions were dominant: his research program was meant to throw light on the causes of business cycles and to assess — in quantitative terms — the effects of certain policy measures (thereby also providing the theory of economic policy with an empirical foundation).

In 1945, Tinbergen was invited by the government, in which the social-democratic Labor Party *(Partij van den Arbeid)* now participated, to set up an economic planning bureau, the Central Planning Bureau (CPB). The planned character of social-economic policy for which the CPB should provide the basic material was, however, of a less strict nature than the word might suggest: the CPB was to develop into a scientific research bureau offering economic *forecasts* and advice. It thus was to play an assistant role in the planning of economic policy. To that purpose, however, it was and is granted an effective amount of independence. Although the planning activities therefore essentially consist of the design of conditional forecasts, these forecasts do play a prominent role in the government's planning activities in the social-economic field: departmental top-staff units heavily rely on these forecasts in their policy designing work, while the CPB is also represented qualitate qua in the most influential and prestigious top civil-service committees and external advisory organs like the Social-Economic Council *(Sociaal-Economische Raad)* (Bemelmans-Videc 1984). Forecasts and advice to benefit options analysis ex ante are also the realm of work of the Social-Cultural Planning Bureau and of the independent external Scientific Council for Government Policy *(Wetenschappelijke Raad voor het Regeringsbeleid)*, the last one specializing in long-term forecasting.

The introduction of policy analysis in its modern sense took place in the early 1970s. Illustrating the increasing consensus on the need for a critical review of government programs and tasks, an interdepartmental Committee for the Development of Policy Analysis *(Commissie voor de Ontwikkeling van Beleidsanalyse — COBA)* was formed by the Minister of Finance. All departments were represented on a high official level, including the CPB and the CBS. The committee was assisted by a (small) staff within the Ministry of Finance.[5]

The committee's tasks were to advise and report to the government (on requests or on its own initiative) about the relevance of policy analysis, to promote the application of policy analysis with the ministries, and to develop appropriate methods. In the years of its existence, COBA has laid heavy emphasis on the clarification of program objectives with the various ministerial departments by developing departmental goal structures (COBA 1979). In these goal structures ("goal trees") abstract program goals are operationalized down to the level of concrete performance indicators. This is, of course, the first thing to do if one attempts to make statements about effectiveness and efficiency. By the end of the 1970s, COBA's own conclusion was that the results of its endeavours in this regard had not been very satisfying; in the majority of the departments the design of goal structures had not yet been completed (COBA 1979). Resistance encountered, in both political and administrative quarters, had been of a familiar nature: explicitly stating policy goals is something of a problem in a multiparty, coalition government system like the Dutch political system. Clarified goals make one vulnerable: politicians are not inclined to show much interest in their own failures.

Even if in these years, politicians would support the idea of policy analysis verbally, actual support would be lacking at crucial moments both on the cabinet and on the departmental level.

Nor are civil servants interested in proving inefficiency and ineffectivity: their careers are also supposed to flourish more by innovation than by reflection on a possibly unsuccessful past. Their hesitation would be stronger with the increasing awareness of the necessity of effecting economies, and with their suspicions that explicit goal structures might pave the way for a program-budgeting system.

Last, but certainly not least, the methodological problems COBA encountered were grave: how to operationalize multiple, changing, conflicting, vague, symbolic, iterative, and qualitative goals, if one succeeds — at all — in creating consensus on the goals of the organization or policy/program.

COBA ended its existence in 1983 and a Department for Policy Analysis *(Afdeling Beleidsanalyse)* was established with the Ministry of Finance that continued COBA's work with regard to consulting activities and education in policy analysis, whose impact on attitudes should not be underrated. The agency's courses in policy evaluation philosophies and techniques for the higher civil service are a necessary complement to the academic education, where training in these arts had been rare until recently.[6]

Of course, an academic training in one of the social and economic sciences, widely represented in the higher civil service, should be fertile soil for the frames of reference associated with policy evaluation methodology. Actual acceptance will of necessity be conditioned by factors like the nature of the policy field and by the political and administrative conditions mentioned above.

The State of Affairs: Policy Evaluation in the Mid-1980s

By the end of the 1970s, the use of policy evaluation ex post with central government was limited. If applied, it would be the more traditional evaluation of administrative practice, the dominant evaluation criterion being lawfulness.

The Committee on the Main Structure of the Government Apparatus *(Commissie Hoofdstructuur Rijksdienst)* had — in its final report, 1980 — come to the same conclusion and had advised that a more institutionalized form of policy evaluation be promoted by applying the idea of sunset legislation (1980, 221).

If one tries to characterize the dominant perceptions and attitudes regarding policy evaluation in the early 1980s, one may do so by indicating that, on the one hand, there was a climate of cynicism, pragmatism, and opportunism (Hoogerwerf 1987, 1); on the other hand, there were clear illustrations of a changing attitude, for example, in changing manners of speaking. Where one used to refuse any form of discipline other than vague and broad criteria for the reviewal of one's work, the idea of program evaluation in its more rigid form became gradually more accepted.

Politicians (ministers and members of Parliament) and top officials were (at least verbally) backing the idea that policy evaluation (of sufficient quality) should be put to use more often. They considered the lack of policy evaluation a problem, for which they — in majority — suggested the solution of institutionalizing evaluation, as the above-mentioned committee had done earlier (Hoogerwerf 1986, 274).

This change in climate was certainly inspired by the economic recession and the ensuring need to economize on government expenditures, a need acknowledged by both the government and the social-democrat opposition.

In recent years, external ad hoc studies have often taken the form of commissioned research, via private contracts in a direct relation between government and a person or institute. There is a rather flourishing market for policy-evaluation research at the moment, apparently attractive to persons and institutes with or without some kind of connection with the academic world.

However, quite a few research projects of evaluatory nature have also been undertaken by academic researchers, financed either directly by their employing academic institute or by government (granting subsidies via research organizations).

The subjects of these studies range over the effects of policy programs on the quality of water, employment, road safety, insurance in case of incapacity to work, and community processes and social participation and technology assessment (see, among others, Beckerand Poreter 1986; Hoogerwerf 1983).

The nature of these research projects may be typified as both program-effect evaluation and administrative-process evaluation.

Then there is also the government-commissioned evaluatory work done by (ad hoc) review committees. There are two recent and interesting examples. The Review Committee on the 1970 Law on University Administrative Reform evaluated it by the four criteria that had been the law's main inspiration: democracy, efficiency, independence, and the promotion of quality of both education and research. The Review Committee on the 1980 Law on the Publicity of Administration concentrated on the evaluation of relevant administrative procedures, and came to rather negative conclusions.

So far as these evaluations had been stipulated in the law itself, they are of an institutionalized nature.

Intradepartmental evaluation ex post is usually limited to (simple) progress reports or more detailed annual reports (Commissie Hoofd-structuur Rijksdienst 1980, 221).

Of course, certain departmental units are — by their very task description — committed to initiate some kind of evaluatory research. Directorates for legislation should be involved in the evaluation of laws, and directorates of financial or economic affairs should promote the introduction and application of policy-analytical methods in relation to the budgetary process (like the performance budget) (Sas 1987, 4).

However, given the nonengaging character of these instructions, actual efforts and their effectiveness will depend largely on the power position of these units in the departmental organization and on actual political backing.

Connected with most ministerial departments are councils or agencies involved in research programming in their respective policy fields, engaging some civil service personnel, but mostly external expertise.

One may conclude that policy evaluation studies are being instigated at all ministerial departments; however they vary greatly as to policy field and as to type and degree of institutionalization (Horrevoets 1984, *iv*). Intradepartmental research is still strongly (sub-) sector-oriented and hardly the kind of research that would facilitate metasector integral reviews and choice. A stimulus for a change in practices and attitudes is the fact that — more than before — Parliament stresses the need for evaluation.

The most prominent example of an institutionalized evaluation procedure of a metadepartmental and relatively systematic character is the so-called Reconsiderations Procedure *(Heroverwegingsoperatie)* that we shall now concentrate on.

The Reconsiderations Procedure

The Reconsiderations Procedure, the most important policy-reviewing operation so far, would inevitably lead to budgetary cuts; there were no doubts left about that from the start.[7]

In the Budget for 1981 (*Miljoenennota 1981*, par. 4.5 pp. 44–45), the government had pointed out that the efforts of the 1970s to realize fundamental reconsideration of government expenditures had failed: proportional cuts had only resulted in letting the air out of departmental budgets, in postponements of expenditures, and in other more or less obvious optical tricks.

Structural changes in policy, based on thorough and rational analysis (as promoted by COBA) had been realized not at all, or only to an insufficient degree. COBA, however, in its educational efforts and methodological work, had paved the way for the operation that the cabinet now deemed necessary: the Reconsiderations Procedure (RP). The cabinet came to the point in a letter from the prime minister to the Second Chamber informing it that instructions had been given to start the analysis and reconsideration of programs and organizations on various fields of policy, and to prepare policy alternatives that would bring about the necessary limitation of growth in government expenditures (Tweede Kamer der S. G. 1980–81, 16625/1, 2).

The instruction was obligatory for all departments, and so were the guidelines for the procedure.

The RP takes place in yearly rounds and is attuned to the budgetary process. In the first round thirty reports came out on thirty subjects, varying from defense policy and the organization of the judicial apparatus, through regional welfare, to public transport.

The selection of subjects for reconsideration is a full-cabinet decision (Parliament is also asked to make its own suggestions). Similarly, the results of the various reconsideration studies are presented to the full cabinet (Verwayen 1984, 2). Selection criteria were also made public in the above-mentioned letter to the Second Chamber, including among others the proportion and growth of a category of expenditure, the possibility of applying the profit principle (the consumer partly paying for a service delivered by the government), and an equal spreading of the subjects over the various chapters of the budget.

The reconsideration studies are carried out by interdepartmental working groups, supervized by civil-service and ministerial top committees, and with secretarial assistance from the Ministry of Finance. The working groups are chaired by the department primarily in charge of the subject under consideration, while other departments participate to the extent of their involvement. The Prime Minister's Office and the Inspectorate of Finance hold seats qualitate qua.

The program focuses on accomplishing the following tasks:

- the description of policy/programs and their objectives, effects, and costs;
- the evaluation of the timeliness, effectiveness, and efficiency of these programs;
- the development of alternatives which would require lower budgetary inputs and the assessment of their effects.

These tasks were specified in the following guidelines for the working groups:

- evaluate the timeliness, effectiveness, and efficiency of policy/program and administrative practice;
- develop three to four less-costly policy alternatives, of which one should lead to savings of at least 20 percent (compared with projected expenditures four years hence: the so-called groan variant);
- find out if this can be achieved via privatization, decentralization, or the application of the profit principle.

Up to and including the seventh round (1987), nearly a hundred evaluation studies had been performed.[8]

Commentators have pointed out the zero-base budgeting approach of the operation that was carried out in considerable depth. The relatively systematic character of the procedure was particularly indicated by the explicitness and uniformity of the guidelines, in which the similarity of the evaluation criteria for all subjects is of special importance. It is far from easy to compare different policy fields with one another in terms applicable to all. Of course, the individual reports differ in quality methodologically and regarding their thoroughness and completeness. And, naturally, participants have been inventive as regards techniques to avoid the operation: by seeking to economize not on the total budget but on the projected growth of the budget, by attempts to delay work, by appealing to the exceptional status of the program or organization under scrutiny, etc. (van Niekerk 1981, 221).

The outcome of the operation has been judged as a relative success, which is considered to be due to the "strait-jacket method" used to give attempts at evasion little chance: the obligatory nature of the procedure, the uniformity in guidelines, a tight time schedule, and the lack of the right to veto by any of the participants (van Niekerk 1981, 216–17). The backbone of the strait-jacket method was — of course — formed by an increasingly grave necessity to effect economies.

A clear indication of the relative success of the RP in terms of its influence on political decision making regarding the budget is the fact that about 25 percent of the results of the RP studies have been used for budgetary cuts, which corresponds to about 30 percent of the cuts in the central-government budget in the 1983–1986 period.[9]

The Reconsiderations Procedure is one of the so-called great operations with (mainly) central government, that include the operations of decentralization, reorganization of the government apparatus, deregulation, privatization, and reduction of the number of government personnel.

The common aim of these operations is to reduce the budget deficit and the great volume of the public sector. In 1983, more than 70 percent of the National Income was spent by or via the public sector. So far, of these great operations, the Reconsideration Procedure has been the most successful (van Nispen and Noordhoek 1986, 22).

The great operations are supposed to reflect the present government's priorities and are illustrative of a feeling of dissatisfaction with the present role of the state: too much interference with too many sectors of social and economic life, overrating of its potential to solve problems, too much inefficiency and bureaucratism, etc. (Tjeenk Willink 1986, 175). No doubt the economic problems, which turned out to be of a structural nature, have been a major inspiration for this change in the political-ideological climate.

Concluding Remarks

In this paper, we have given a survey of the main actors involved in and institutional arrangements created for the evaluation of (central-)government policy/programs in the Netherlands, while also indicating the state of affairs in policy evaluation.

The introduction of policy-evaluation practices in the modern sense took place in the early 1970s with the establishment of an interdepartmental committee that would concentrate on the analysis of departmental goal structures. This attempt to apply policy-analytical methods in order to improve the quality of political choice was to encounter resistance from both political and administrative quarters. The increasing pressure of a deteriorating economic and financial situation, resulting in the necessity of reducing the budget deficit, would gradually stimulate political interest and backing for evaluatory research. That was clearly illustrated by the Reconsiderations Procedure, where evaluation studies were required to provide a basis for political decisions regarding the reallocation of money.

Notes

1. Re government subsidies for the sectors of ship building and house building.
2. "Administrative organization" should be read as the management information system.
3. The fact-finding procedure is the crucial point of advice that the Second Chamber gave in this report in which it critically analyzed its own organization and procedures.
4. Supplementary legislation to the *Comptabiliteitswet*, Staatsblad 1986, 605.
5. COBA (and now the Department Policy Analysis) issues a quarterly periodical, *Beleidsanalyse* (*Policy Analysis*), in which may be found articles and reports on the state of the art, at home and abroad.

6. In the curricula of the recently established academic specializations in public administration, policy analysis is one of the main topics.
7. Sincere thanks are due to Mrs. G. Bruin, who provided us with relevant quantitative data on the results of the Reconsiderations Procedure, and to Mr. Ed Borst for his background research on the subject.
8. As from the fifth round in the procedure, instructions about the evaluatory part of the studies had become less strict, while emphasis was being put on the development of less-costly policy alternatives.
9. *Miljoenennota 1983*, p. 107. Nonofficial sources state percentages varying from 20 to 30 percent.

References

Arvidsson, G. 1986. "Performance evaluation." Pp. 625–643 in *Guidance, control, and evaluation in the public sector*. Berlin: Walter de Gruyter. New York: The Bielefeld Interdisciplinary Project.

Becker, H. A., and A. L. Porter, eds. 1986. *Impact assessment today*. Vol. 1 and 2. Utrecht: Van Arkel.

Bemelmans-Videc, M. L. 1984. *Economen in overheidsdienst*. Leiden/Rotterdam.

Braband, van W. J. 1987. *Rekenkameronderzoek en Budgetrecht*. Een pleidooi voor beleidsrapportages, in Macht en onmacht van bestuurlyke evaluaties, Geschriften van de Vereniging voor Bestuurskunde, Congrespublikahes.

COBA. 1979. *Beleidsanalyse* 2:4–6.

Commissie Hoofdstructuur Rijksdienst. 1980. Rapport nr. 3. *Elk kent de laan die derwaart gaat*. Den Haag.

Hoogerwerf, A., ed. 1983. *Succes en falen van overheidsbeleid*. Samson, Alpen a.d. Rÿn.

Hoogerwerf, A., 1986. *Vanaf de top geaien*; Visies van de politieke elite. Amsterdam: Sÿthoff.

————. 1987. *Departementale beleidsevaluatie; In leiding en probleemstelling*. Congresbijdrage Vereniging voor Bestuurskunde.

Horrevoets, M. S. G. 1984. *Beleidsevaluatie op rijksniveau*. Een peiling van recente ontwikkelingen. Delft: Planologisch Studiecentrum TNO.

Miljoenennota. 1981.

————. 1983.

Niekerk van, N. C. M. 1981. "Heroverwegingsopratie 1981 en het ambacht van ombuigen." *Openbare Uitgaven* 13 (5).

Nispen van, F. K. M., and D. P. Noordhoek. 1986. *De grote operaties*. De overheid onder het mes of het snijden in eigen vlees, Deventer: Kluwer.

Rijn, A. 1983. In Hoogerwerf 1986.

Sas, C. 1987. *Beleidsevaluaties binnen de Rijksdienst*. Congresbijdrage Vereniging voor Bestuurskunde.

Tjeenk Willink, H. D. 1986. "Samenhang grote operaties." P. 175 in van Nispen and Noordhoek 1986.

Tweede Kamer der S. G. 1980–81. 16625, nr. 1. *Heroverweging collectieve uitgaven*. Brief van de minister-president an de Tweede Kamer, dd. 11 Februari 1981.

Tweede Kamer der S. G. 1985–86. 19336, nrs. 1 en 2. *Rapport onderzoek van de organisatie en de werkwijze der Kamer.*

Verwayen, Drs. H. 1984. "Policy review and budgeting: Some experiences with the 'Reconsiderations Procedure' in the Netherlands." OECD paper on policy-review processes and budgeting, 29 June 1984.

7

Institutional Aspects of
Evaluation in Norway

Bjarne Eriksen

Introduction

The term "evaluation" will be used in a very broad sense in the following discussion. The area of interest includes evaluation of central government programs and measures at various levels, whether comprehensive or limited in scope.

Another consideration that should be mentioned at the outset is the fact that evaluation is not always carried out in its pure form. It is often combined with other activities, for instance, in the case of research assignments.

As a background for the description which follows, it may be useful to take a brief look at the way in which evaluation has evolved. This may serve as a particularly useful point of departure for discussion as to who takes the initiative for evaluation.

Until just a few years ago the main emphasis was on planning, with little attention given to evaluation. There are several reasons for the present greatly increased interest in evaluation of government programs and measures.

Why the Increased Emphasis on Evaluation?

Limited Economic Resources

It is obvious that in a time of limited economic resources there will be a growing interest in the effectiveness of government measures. In other words, the desired goal is to get the most for the money, so the question of the efficiency and effectiveness of government spending is raised. As large shares of the gross national product are used in the public sector, it is even more important to justify the use of these funds.

It should also be mentioned that changes in society demand a strengthening of some sectors and a decrease in others.

Service to the General Public

The question is raised as to the quality of the service rendered by government administration to the public. In considering these issues, it is only natural that there is an increasing demand for more systematic evaluation of government programs. Information material and guidelines for such evaluation have been produced. One such publication is called *The general public—A source of feedback for government administration*; a second publication is called *A handbook in studies of the public's reactions*.[1]

Organization of Government Services

Another factor contributing to the increasing demand for evaluation is related to the structure of government administration. Decentralization and delegation of authority are a strong trend at present. The emphasis is on goal-oriented and result-oriented management. Thus evaluation is an important element in the feedback process.

Improved Productivity

The 1980s have seen an emphasis on improved productivity in government administration. A productivity campaign was carried out in 1982 in both government administration and the private sector. A natural component of such productivity efforts is the evaluation of results, in the form of measuring productivity.

Evaluation of Interrelated Sectors

Another factor to be mentioned is related to the need for evaluation across agency and sector boundaries. It is reasonable that each individual institution or sector concentrates on evaluation of its own activities, but it is also evident that an evaluation that gives a highly positive result in one sector may give a highly negative result in another sector. An example that may serve to illustrate this problem is the relation between the agricultural, transport, and energy sectors in the light of the environmental sector.

Fertilization in agriculture may give very good results in terms of productivity within agriculture, but it may contribute to pollution of the water in adjacent water systems.

Simplification of Regulations

The desire to simplify regulations is another contributory factor. There seems to be a consensus that government regulations have become too comprehensive, incomprehensible, and complicated, and there is a call for simplification. In this connection the question of evaluation arises. How does the present set of regulations work, and what may be the effect of altering these regulations?

Who Takes the Initiative for Evaluation?

The initiative for evaluation, whether direct or indirect, may come from a number of quarters. The most important ones are mentioned in the following subsections.

Initiatives from the Parliament and the Government

A number of sectors and institutions are required by law or administrative decision to send regular reports to the Parliament (Storting). These reports include, among other things, some evaluation.

The proposition to the Storting (January 1985), which formed the basis for reforms in the central government budgetary system, states:

> It is prescribed that central government agencies shall draw up operational plans on the basis of approved funding. These plans shall indicate what resources are intended to be used for the agency's various tasks. Systems must be worked out for reporting during the current period in which results are examined in relation to the budgetary aims. Major agencies must draw up departmental budgets and departmental accounts. Each agency must develop its own systems for measuring results, as appropriate to its activities.[2]

The Funding Regulations *(Bevilgningsreglementet)* which have been laid down by the Storting state:

> The results that are intended shall be described in the budget proposition. . . .

> Information concerning results achieved during the previous accounting year shall be included in the budget proposition in question, along with other accounting information that is significant for an evaluation of the budget proposition for the coming year.[3]

A royal decree (1985) states that administrative and economic consequences of law proposals, etc., should be elucidated.

A general initiative for evaluation might be taken in connection with special measures. Two such special measures in the 1980s are

- the 1982 Productivity Campaign;
- the plan of action for user-minded public services.

The Ministries and Their Agencies

The initiative for evaluation is taken by the ministries in many instances. However, such initiatives may also come from other levels within government administration, for example, from a directorate or an institute.

Committees, Etc.

In connection with major studies, specially appointed review committees will take the initiative for evaluation. These committees may conduct evaluations themselves, or they may assign the task of evaluation to others.

Research Institutions

In addition to the evaluation task researchers are assigned by government administration, they themselves also initiate research concerning evaluation of central government programs and measures.

Others

Others who may take the initiative for evaluations include:

- special interest organizations;
- other nongovernment organizations;
- the Office of the Auditor General;
- the Central Bureau of Statistics;
- the Directorate of Organization and Management.

Who Conducts Evaluations?

Evaluations can take many forms, from simple user inquiries to comprehensive scientific studies. Use inquiries have become very commonplace and are implemented in many situations. As mentioned above, guidelines for such studies have been drawn up, and the studies are often conducted by government administration itself, as well as by commissioned research institutions or private firms.

The Ministries

In terms of the more comprehensive evaluations, the ministries naturally play a central role. There are no special evaluation departments in the ministries, but planning and research departments were established particularly during the 1960s and 1970s. The study which formed the basis for establishing many of these departments (1970) states that, among other activities, they are to:

- analyze and evaluate economic and social developments within the ministry's sphere of activities on the basis of alternative premises, and evaluate the consequent choices for ministry policy;
- identify the aims on which ministry policy can be based;
- work for the development and implementation of better methods in ministry planning, such as cost analyses, program analyses and cost-benefits analyses;
- have responsibility for an overall evaluation of the ministry's need for information, in terms of both statistical data and research. This may also include initiatives for the production of more comprehensive and relevant information, for example, through commissioned studies.[4]

An examination of the activities specified indicates that evaluation is one of them. Only to a limited extent will the planning departments themselves conduct evaluations. To a great extent, they will commission others to do so, particularly research institutions.

The planning department in the newest ministry, the Ministry of Development Cooperation, has a separate division for evaluation and research. The proposition to the Storting which laid the basis for the establishment of this ministry in 1983 states that

> Evaluation of aid programs will also be an important dimension of planning, in order to ensure that there is correspondence between aims and the practical work of achieving them. The close relation between overall planning and the implementation of general recommendations in evaluation reports will be ensured by placing the responsibility for evaluation in the planning department.

> Responsibility for research will also be placed in the planning department, in part because of the need for close contact between research and evaluation.

> The planning department will consist of two planning divisions having a total of twelve positions. The First Planning Division will be responsible for questions of policy and of a more general nature, allocation of funds amongst the

main budgetary items, coordination of participation in the Nordic senior officials' committee for development cooperation (EKB) and the development assistance committee of the OECD (DAC). The Second Planning Division will be responsible for the administration of evaluation and research.[5]

As regards the ministries, it should also be mentioned that a report from the Directorate of Public Management called *The ministries' supervision and use of research; An investigation based on the Ministry of Health and Social Affairs* (1986)[6] sets forth a number of proposals to improve the use and supervision of research. They deal with research in general, but will also apply to research having to do with evaluation.

The report states in part:

Internal organization and working methods

We recommend that contributions in this area by senior officials should be increased. A means of achieving this is to establish a permanent committee for research, studies, and pilot projects. The heads of department should be members of this committee, which should be responsible for coordinating initiatives, making recommendations as to allocations, and carrying on a dialogue with the political leadership. Consideration should be given to whether the meetings of the directors general can fill this role.

Measures should be taken to facilitate the personnel's contact with research being done throughout the ministry on a broad basis. This is elaborated with further proposals in four areas.
1) The use of contact persons for projects and programs should be increased.
2) Internal researchers in short-term engagements should be better utilized.
3) The possibilities for exchanging personnel with research institutions should be extended.
4) Improvement of the personnel's competence oriented towards research, studies, and pilot projects should become a part of personnel and leadership training in the ministry.

Agencies under the Ministries

There are also agencies under the auspices of the ministries that have planning divisions or other divisions which either conduct evaluations themselves or cooperate with others, for example, research institutions. The Directorate of Public Management to some extent conducts evaluations in connection with administrative development projects.

Review Committees

Review committees also conduct evaluations. A good example is the study by the committee to investigate internal supervision in an overall strategy for the working environment and safety (NOU 1987, 10A). The committee's mandate states that the committee is also

> to chart and evaluate the experiences to date (positive/negative effects) seen from the point of view of the authorities, the companies and the workforce, describe and evaluate the development of the models and their mode of operation (intended and unintended effects), and hereunder to assess administrative and financial consequences.[7]

Research Institutions

A vast amount of evaluation is carried out by research institutions. This is true of various types of research institutions: within the social sciences, the natural sciences, agriculture, fisheries, etc. It is often the large-scale evaluation studies that are conducted by research institutions.

Activities of the Research Councils

In terms of assessment within research, it is largely the research councils which conduct evaluations. According to Report Proposition No. 6 (1984–85) to the Storting on research in Norway:

> The research councils have three primary responsibilities: research strategy, financing, and evaluation. The research councils are now revising their evaluation routines, and parts of the research system have been evaluated by foreign experts. The research councils should continue to examine their routines for the purpose of becoming better able to function as bodies of research strategy and evaluation.[8]

Private Firms

Private consulting firms in particular may be commissioned to conduct evaluations. For instance, when the productivity campaign was launched in 1982, private consulting firms were engaged to undertake evaluations.

Individuals

Individuals with special competence, who are authorities on evaluation, may also be commissioned to conduct evaluations.

The Supreme Audit Institution of Norway

The functions and activities of the auditor general are related to the evaluation of policies and programs. The short description given in this paragraph is quoted from:

The supreme audit institution of Norway—Functions and activities. Oslo 1986.[9]

Origin and Background

The Office of the Auditor General (OAG) is the controlling agency of the Norwegian Parliament — the Storting. Its origin goes back to the Norwegian Constitution of 1814 which provides that the Storting, for its four year term, shall elect five auditors general with a mandate to examine the annual financial statements of the government which make up the Public Accounts of Norway.

These five auditors general, one of whom is designated as chairman of the group, constitute the Board of the Auditors General, with overall directive and supervisory authority in all matters of general policy. Responsibility for the day-to-day management of the organization rests with the chairman.

Within the constitutional structure of government, OAG has always been part of the legislative branch. It stands independent of the executive branch and is answerable and subservient only to the legislature, that is, the Storting.

The OAG, which internationally might be referred to as the Supreme Audit Institution (SAI), is in Norway organized into five operation departments plus one administrative section.

Financial Auditing

It is still an important part of OAG's responsibilities to examine the annual financial statements of the government, and to prepare and publish certified extracts of the Public Accounts of the nation.

This requires and presupposes a continuing process of current examinations and audits throughout the year of accounts and records of individual government entities (departments, agencies, institutions, etc.), all of which ultimately are to be included or reflected in the Public Accounts.

In earlier periods much effort went into painstakingly examining individual transactions, to see whether they were properly documented and authorized and correctly recorded. However, the growing scope and complexity of government operations, in Norway as well as in most other countries, have made such auditing methods largely impractical or even impossible. Also, the individual "detail approach" has become less necessary as departments and agencies, encouraged by OAG, have established internal auditing routines of their own coupled with improved financial management and better control procedures.

Today, the financial audit is directed towards verifying that accounting procedures and financial statements conform to the stated accounting policies and principles of the government, and that

- individual transactions are duly authorized and correctly recorded;
- accounts and statements properly and reliably reflect the underlying actual dispositions;
- accounts and statements give a true informative picture of the economic results for the period covered.

Performance Audit

In performance auditing the emphasis is less on the amount of public expenditures and more on how and with what results the funds were spent. Performance auditing involves a systematic evaluation of overall use and management of public funds and assets, based on a critical analysis of objectives, use of resources, and results achieved. Financial and performance audits must not be viewed as mutually exclusive or contradictory, but rather as complementary. Traditional financial auditing will often provide a good and even necessary starting point for the more extensive and intensive performance audit.

Advisory Activities

When irregular or doubtful dispositions have been uncovered, OAG may find it expedient and also sufficient to advise corrective measures for the future. The same limited reaction may also be suitable in cases where internal control routines and work procedures are unsatisfactory or need improvement.

In this respect, OAG can act as a channel of information, by being able to provide government entities and offices with advisory circulars and guidelines prepared by special consultative agencies. It will also make available, where needed, its own knowledge of and experience with systems, procedures, and routines that have been observed to work properly and satisfactorily elsewhere.

Monitoring Public Grants

The annual budget usually provides for sizable grant appropriations to public-sector activities, to semipublic and private organizations, and to private individuals.

Grants of this type for the benefit of public or private activities not directly subject to government control are given with the reservation and the understanding that the originating agency and OAG both shall have the right to check and verify that the funds are being used for the purpose intended.

Auditing Government Enterprises, Companies, and Banks

Some government enterprises are in reality instruments of public policy and are part and parcel of the government administration itself, with revenues and expenditures included in the budget and in the financial statements of the government. Enterprises of this type are mostly part of the economic infrastructure of the country, such as railroads, postal services, telecommunications, electric power systems, etc. The activities and the accounts of these entities are subject to the same type of OAG audit as are the traditional government agencies.

Reporting to the Storting

The results and conclusions based on the OAG audit of the government's financial statements and on the continuous audit throughout the year of the individual departments and numerous agencies, institutions, and other entities are presented annually in a final report, officially designated as Document No. 1. The report is normally submitted to the Storting in the fall after the summer recess, and covers the preceding fiscal calendar year.

The Central Bureau of Statistics

The functions and activities of the Central Bureau of Statistics also relate to evaluation. The following material is a quotation from the information pamphlet *This is the Central Bureau of Statistics*, 1983.[10]

The Central Bureau of Statistics was established as an independent institute in 1876 and has ever since been the central agency for the compilation of official Norwegian statistics. It defines its main tasks as establishing which statistics and analyses there is a need for in society, developing and maintaining a system of official statistics, and employing statistics in the analysis of important social questions.

The institution also has the special duties of carrying out research into taxation and analysis of international economic trends. The Bureau also has an administrative function as the central office of population registration. Population censuses, and later population and housing censuses, which have been taken roughly every tenth year since 1769, are an important part of the Bureau's work.

Some of the publications are intended to shed light on particular topics, while others survey a variety of topics, a period of time, or the like. The Statistical Yearbook and Historical Statistics are good examples of publications containing statistics relating to several fields. The publications also contain time series.

The production of statistics and analyses by the Central Bureau of Statistics can be divided into three main fields:

• Economic statistics and analyses relating to subjects in such fields as social, industrial, and business economics. Such statistics include statistics for domestic and foreign trade, the national accounts, and price, wage, and building-cost indexes.
• Sociodemographic statistics and analyses which describe the population and such important factors relating to it as health, education, social and living conditions, and welfare.
• Statistics relating to resources and the environment, which provide information on our natural resources and their management.

Who Pays for Evaluations?

In some instances, special funding may be appropriated for evaluation. This may be particularly in connection with special pilot projects, investigations, studies, etc.

Normally, however, funding for evaluations has to be taken from the ordinary budget. Such funding may consist of earmarked funds for research, inquiries, use of private consultants, etc.

Reports, Etc.

Reports are submitted to the Storting concerning activities in certain institutions and sectors. These reports also include some evaluations. The system of reports to the Storting was reviewed by a committee and finally debated in the Storting in 1985. The result was that the number of institutions and sectors to submit reports to the Storting was reduced; only certain institutions and sectors may, now submit reports.

In addition to these reports, the Storting receives reports via the annual budget proposition. These reports are also to contain comments on the results attained.

Reports from review committees are normally published in a series called Norway's Official Reports (NOU).

The documents mentioned above—that is, reports to the Storting, budget propositions, other propositions, and NOU—are documents that are readily available and that can be purchased by the general public.

In addition to the mentioned official reports and documents, special evaluation reports are produced, some of which are published, whereas others remain within the sector involved.

Conclusion

As pointed out in the above pages there is a growing interest in evaluation of government programs and measures. This can also be read out of the government's renewal program, where more emphasis is placed on goal-achievement that necessitates more evaluation and reporting of results.

Problems of evaluation are however many sided, and may be looked at from different angles. To mention some:

• The politicians and the administrators have different needs.
• The different levels of administration also have different needs.
• There are a great number of different methods to be used.
• Some evaluation results are of immediate interest, while others have a long-term interest.
• There is often a long time lag between evaluation and the evaluation results being used.

Up to now, evaluation endeavors have been rather fragmentary. In the future, there will be a need for better planning and much more systematic work at all levels in order to have good evaluation and efficient use made of the evaluation results.[11]

Notes

1. *Håndbok i publikumsundersøkelser* Universitetsforlaget, Oslo. (Handbook in studies of the public's reactions). 1984.
2. St.pr. nr. 52. 1984–85. *Om reformer i budsjettsystem og endringer i bevilgningsreglement* (About reforms of the budget system and alterations of the Funding Regulations).
3. *Bevilgningsreglementet* (The Funding Regulations) Laid down by the Parliament (*Stortinget*).
4. *Innstilling om planleggings- og budsjetteringsorganene i staten* (Report about planning and budgeting organs in government administration). 1970.
5. St.prp. nr. 1. Tillegg nr. 1. 1983–84. for budsjetterminen. 1984. *Om opprettelse av Departementet for utviklingshjelp* (About the establishment of the Ministry of the Development Cooperation).

6. *Departementenes styring og bruk av forskning* (The ministries steering and use of research). Report from the Directorate of Public Management, 1986.
7. Norwegian Public Reports — NOU 1987: 10A. Internal control in an integrated strategy for working environment and safety.
8. St.meld. nr. 60. 1984–85. *Om forskningen i Norge* (About research in Norway).
9. *The Supreme Audit Institution of Norway: Functions & Activities.* 1986. Pamphlet issued by the Office of the Auditor General of Norway, Oslo.
10. *This is the Central Bureau of Statistics.* 1983. Pamphlet issued by the Central Bureau of Statistics, Oslo.
11. Survey issued by Royal Norwegian Ministry of Consumer Affairs and Government Administration. 1988. Department of Planning and Information Technology, Oslo.

8

Switzerland: Moving towards Evaluation

Katia Horber-Papazian and Laurent Thévoz

Introduction

If evaluation is taken as being an attempt to explain the outcomes of legislation or a policy, and to measure its effectiveness and efficiency against preset objectives, it must be admitted that evaluation of this kind is uncommon in Switzerland. Which is effectively to say that the Swiss system currently contains few evaluative processes operated to formal, explicitly stated rules.

And yet evaluation does occur in the form of the expressly provided control mechanisms applied by a variety of agencies. But that type of evaluation appears to be inadequate and ineffectual in coping either with the new demands emerging from a spectrum of political outlooks or the increase in volume and complexity of state programs to be implemented. These various factors raise four main questions, which the present paper seeks to answer:

- What features peculiar to the Swiss politico-administrative system condition the implementation of all public policies?
- How has the system operated to date with regard to evaluation?
- Why and by whom have doubts been raised about the existing machinery?
- How is evaluation of legislation and public policy to enter the Swiss system?

Description of the Swiss System

The peculiarities of the Swiss system arise out of its politico-administrative framework (federalism, local implementation, and "subsidiarity" or last-resort intervention), its political culture based on consensus, and its financial rigor. These characteristics may be at once assets and liabilities in the implementation of public policies.

Federalism

The Confederation, cantons (26), and communes or municipalities (3,029) are all units of government with autonomous, historically established powers (Knapp 1987) deriving from their own legal, financial, political, and human rights and resources.

Given that, all — or nearly all — federal policies require cooperation between authorities from all three tiers of government who must be capable of intervening throughout the implementation process.

The areas in which the Confederation has exclusive jurisdictional autonomy are limited to defense, foreign policy, and external trade policy.

The communal (municipal) and cantonal authorities are very close to their publics in the geographical, social, and electoral senses. The resources available to these subnational governments enables the needs of the population and special interest groups to be taken into account and met at the lowest levels of administration.

This local government autonomy frequently leads to new federal laws being passed after cantonal or communal ordinances covering the same matter, producing a situation in which the overlay of public policies deriving from different levels of government leads to an intermeshing, if not a contradiction in objectives and means, which can only be untangled or reconciled with difficulty (Morand 1987).

Local Implementation

By "local implementation" we mean the rule by which — save in very rare instances — cantons have the power to make decisions and implement federal policy locally, in the great majority of cases with federal funds. As a general rule, there are no decentralized federal agencies operating at cantonal or communal level to accomplish, direct, and supervise the application of federal laws.

The Confederation's ability to step in and take over from a canton which has failed to perform its implementing tasks represents the federal government's chief concurrent right over the application of federal laws. While that right is very rarely exercised, the Confederation may, by contrast, request any federally aided canton to report on its activities.

The advantage of this implementing federalism is the ability, where cooperation exists between the authorities and where pressure groups are favorable to the policy followed, to adapt implementation of federal laws to space- and time-specific cases and situations.

Where a federal law is an outline law, or merely reserves ultimate policy supervision powers to the Confederation, then that alone devolves full implementing responsibility to the cantons.

Subsidiarity, or (Last-Resort Intervention)

The principle of subsidiarity, widely accepted and applied in Switzerland, effectively provides that government will not intervene to meet an identified social need unless and until civil society (in the form of individuals, private organizations, associations, or market forces) have proved manifestly incapable of responding to it. The further consequence of that is that the federal government will not assume a responsibility which can be assumed by the communes, the cantons, or both. The same principle governs relations between canton and commune. The simplicity and clarity of this principle, however, falls down over the difficulty of ensuring adherence to it in all cases of public-authority intervention.

Consensus

To lessen the risk of referenda and assure institutional stability, the Swiss system endeavors to come to terms with (almost) all interests and to attract the support of the great majority. This is not made any easier by the fragmentation of Swiss society by language divisions (French, German, Italian, and Romansch), religious divisions (Protestant and Catholic), political differences (a dozen or so parties), and marked regional disparities.

To obtain a consensus, the federal government embarks on consultation with cantons and with leading established associations and interest groups. This consultation, of vital importance in the preparation of legislation, is supplemented by consultation channeled through a network of extra-parliamentary committees. Some 10 percent of the 370 or so committees of this type are involved in the preparation of legislation. The composition of these committees is: 21.6 percent federal administrators, 20.5 percent cantonal and communal representatives, 22.1 percent business-representatives, and 11.3 percent university representatives (Germann and Fruttiger 1981).

It is at these different levels that compromises are negotiated and consensus is forged, the price for the latter being guarantees that each party's interests will be taken into account on the one hand, and the assurance of public support on the other — sometimes at the expense of a solution to the real underlying problem.

Financial Rigor

Switzerland has a time-honored, all-pervading attachment to savings and the containment of public spending. The influence of this tradition is hard to pin down in any practical sense; nonetheless it manifests itself, diffusely but in a real sense, throughout all levels of all public agencies. The effect has been to instill in government agencies and the public alike, as an item of faith, the principle that a sound policy is a low-cost policy or one unlikely to produce a deficit in the local authority budget. This attitude finds concrete expression in federal, cantonal, and communal fiscal legislation setting public agencies the medium-term objective of balancing their budgets. It is open to question, however, whether the quest for financial break-even at all costs does not in fact lead to budget cuts whose effect is to jeopardize and cast doubt on the implementation of centrally decided measures.

The Machinery of Control

How, in the context described above, are comprehensive policies to be conducted, needs appraised, objectives defined, and the steps taken towards attaining them monitored, target publics identified, and resources determined; most of all, how are we to evaluate whether the expected outcomes have been attained or not, whether the results are due to the efforts made or other factors, and whether the resources mobilized have been deployed to good purpose?

Do the available methods of control fulfill those functions?

Parliamentary Control of Government Activity

The Federal Assembly (Parliament) is composed of two chambers, the National Council (two hundred members elected directly, generally for four years, by proportional representation) and the Council of States (forty-six members representing the cantons, elected by majority vote for four years). The Federal Assembly is the supreme supervisory agency of federal government and management. Both chambers have identical powers, and statutes are passed by assent of both chambers.

The Parliament elects the federal government, which comprises seven members drawn from the four largest parties: the Radicals (Liberals), the Socialists, the Christian Democrats, and the Center Democrates (People's Party), which between them represent some 85 percent of all votes.

The government is collectively responsible for its decisions, and is the supreme managerial and executive authority of the Confederation. It directs federal business and public administration, and exercises constant supervision over the administrative system (Aubert 1967).

The Assembly has various methods of control at its disposal:

- questions or challenges to members of the executive branch;
- requests that the government examine whether particular measures should not be adopted;
- motions calling upon the government to take certain steps;
- the creation of parliamentary committees as watchdogs to monitor developments in specific issue or sectors;
- management committees in both chambers; these are Parliament's chief means of control.

These committees enable the Federal Assembly to examine past activities (after-the-event control) of the Federal Council and the administrative and judicial branches, chiefly to determine whether the authorities concerned have correctly discharged the responsibilities devolved to them by the Constitution and by statute, and whether the decisions taken are politically timely and advisable (Mastronardi 1987).

The government also lays before the Federal Assembly a detailed annual report on its management of federal business, in addition to which it must prepare an entirely separate report on measures put into effect and the actual outcomes in specific areas of exclusive jurisdiction (assistance to universities, external economic measures, international humanitarian aid, and agricultural policy).

These various controls are limited by factors inherent to the separation of powers, the type of controls implemented, and the characteristics of Parliament.

Separation of powers Its examination once completed, the Federal Assembly can only accept the report submitted to it or request further information on any particular matter. It could virtually refuse to accept political responsibility for the decisions taken, but has no powers whatever to squash a decision. Its role is confined to pointing out mistakes and illegalities and drawing the government's attention to them.

Type of control The Federal Assembly operates after-the-event controls, chiefly regarding opportuneness; these therefore vary with the political majority and current trends in thinking.

Characteristics of Parliament Parliament is a body of nonspecialists which, given the complexity of the matters before it and the limited time available, does not always have the resources to carry out its supervisory duty and finds itself obliged to devolve the lion's share of its control duties to parliamentary committees. The dispersion of supervision among different committees produces a lack of coherence in supervision policy and, given the volume of work, leads to control very much on a case-by-case basis (Mader 1985).

Financial Control

Switzerland has no Court of Audit. Financial supervision is handled by a relatively independent division of the Department of Finance: the Financial Control Division.

Parliamentary control over finances is exercised by a finance committee for each chamber and a standing committee, the Office of the Delegate for Finance.

The chief criteria for financial control lie in the justifications of expenditure and compliance with their statutory basis.

The main liability of this form of financial control — and it is a substantial one — is its failure to address the question of variance from the objectives of expenditure, or to permit any genuine questioning of expenditure. This drawback is inherent to the type of control applied and the paucity of information available to the controlling agencies.

Administrative Control

Tentative experiments with policy evaluation have been tried by the federal administration (road safety, old-age insurance), but currently operated administrative controls reflect a preoccupation with rationalization, practicability, and the efficacy of administrative activities more than a concern with the effects of central government measures whose implementation is often in the hands of different departments and authorities. This can partly be explained by the poor information flow between departments and layers of government (federal, cantonal, and communal), and partly by the additional work load that evaluation means for an administrative system with a virtually zero-growth establishment.

Judicial Control

Judicial controls are exercised by the cantonal courts and the Federal Tribunal (a court of final resort, one of whose chief tasks is to ensure the unified application of federal law).

The purpose of this judicial control is chiefly to ensure that the administration does not exceed its legal power and does not infringe on personal freedoms. These controls are exercised only in legal proceedings, and are thus merely case-by-case controls. Chiefly concerned with whether the law has been validly applied (that is, concerned with constitutionality and legality), they do not address the question of opportuneness, and only very occasionally do they allow for measurement of the true impacts of norms in social reality (too few controls on too few occasions) (Mader 1985).

Federal Supervision of Cantons

In the majority of cases, the Confederation formulates the broad outlines of laws, and cantons put them into effect.

The Federal Council, or the appropriate departments, have the power to monitor implementation by requesting activity reports from the implementing authority. These reports are most usually called for in areas of federally aided activity. If irregularities are found to have occurred, the responsible central department will ask the canton to rectify it. The Confederation can exert financial pressure on recalcitrant cantons (withdrawal of grants or of their share of federal revenues) or even implement the policy on behalf of the canton. These sanctions are rarely applied.

Political Control by the Citizenry

In a semi-direct democracy such as Switzerland, citizens have a number of political rights. In addition to freedom of expression through elections and ballots, Swiss citizens can also make their views known through petitions, referenda, and initiatives.

Referenda Referenda at cantonal and federal levels are compulsory for amendments to the Constitution. In contrast, federal referenda are optional for legislation, and are held only where requisitioned by fifty thousand electors or eight cantons (optional referenda are requisitioned for some 10 percent of statutes).

Initiatives The right of initiative enables voters in cantons to propose laws and legislative and constitutional amendments. Federal initiatives exist only for constitutional amendments. One hundred thousand signatures are required for a total or partial revision of the Constitution (only three initiatives have been accepted by the electorate since 1891.)

These two important rights allow Swiss citizens to veto proposed parliamentary bills, to force popular consultation by way of referenda, and, in the case of initiatives, to prompt the authorities to address previously ignored problems. While such manifestations of public opinion enable the legislature to take the pulse of the nation or reveal the existence of a problem, they provide no real feedback on government initiatives in that they emerge in an indeterminate manner on specific problems evinced by disparate special interest groups.

Comments

The various mechanisms described above show that, in Switzerland, evaluation (if evaluation there be) is first and foremost after-the-event control of legality or opportuneness, and very rarely control of efficiency or effectiveness. This is equally true at all levels of government — federal, cantonal, and communal. This type of control provides only an incomplete picture of the impacts of centrally determined measures, and only in rare cases does it resolve the problems of public policy formulation and implementation.

Very generally prompted by a ground swell of public opinion (calls for information by organized groups or by the opposition), the evaluation undertaken, or whatever type, is applied only on a spot basis to meet actual problems, doubts, or crises. Conducted by administrators or extra-parliamentary committees, its rules are imprecise and rarely formalized.

Descriptive of a situation at a given moment in time, it offers only a superficial diagnosis in the absence of a complete checkup. Moreover, it works on the assumption that positive-control results (for example, lawfulness, opportune policy, no cost overrun) indicate a sound policy which must, perforce, have the desired outcomes. The measure-to-outcome link is thus considered to be direct. But our brief sketch of the peculiarities of the Swiss politico-administrative system has revealed that its complexity, coupled with the intermeshing of responsibilities, gives considerable cause for doubting the validity of that assumption, chiefly on the following grounds.

- The Confederation has limited power to conduct a comprehensive policy on its own; that is, it relies on the implementing actors.
- The implementing actors are close to the target public. While highly favorable to the implementation of cantonal and communal policies, that very closeness may, when it comes to federal policies, lead to the policy objectives being interpreted in the light of local interests and hence to a diversion of its primary objectives.
- The intermeshing federal and cantonal objectives occasionally conflict.
- It is difficult, because of the need for consensus, to set clear objectives directly referable to the problem at hand and to the needs of those affected.

Together, these problems highlight the need for the politico-administrative system to develop formalized machinery for evaluation, to be used systematically and unambiguously at all stages from the making of public policy to analysis of its impacts.

But is the political climate conducive to such an approach?

A Political Climate Conducive to Evaluation

The growing complexity of government tasks and the problems to be addressed leave the citizen feeling increasingly "left out and left behind".

The citizen has three available options: be resigned to the fact, continue to have confidence in the authorities, or call the authorities to account. For decades, the Swiss have had confidence and closed ranks, and nothing seemed about to change that.

Two major incidents in Swiss political life upset this particular apple cart, however. The first was the 1964 "Mirage" affair. A massive overexpenditure for the purchase of Mirage fighter aircraft, disclosed by the government to the Federal Assembly, brought home to the parliamentarians the extent of their dependence on the federal executive, particularly with regard to information, and they resolved to strengthen their means of control (Urio 1972).

The second incident occurred in the 1970s when, following the approval of an initiative to halt all foreign immigration into Switzerland, the Swiss had to face up to their new image as xenophobes. These crises brought latent conflicts to a head, throwing the sometimes highly rose-tinted image of Switzerland into question (Reszler 1986).

The discontent, initially confined to a few lone voices crying in the wilderness, swelled with the economic crisis into a broader debate just as the federal, cantonal, and communal executives were acquiring wider tasks in economic, social, transport, and environmental policy. The questioning of the choices made, the desire to contain public spending, the year of state interference in too many areas (such as health and agriculture), and fierce opposition to federal policy planning (for example, national trunk roads) or constrictive policies (such as energy policy) saw the role of the state and the technocrats being questioned in an increasing number of circles.

The Right wants to "roll back the state," the Left seeks "a more caring state." Proponents of both views need arguments to back up their claims. But arguments are built on information about state activities and their outcomes, the effectiveness and efficiency of lawfully taken decisions. This quest for information is reflected in Parliament by questions and motions addressed to the government. The answers received often appear very vague and inadequate. At the same time, a wind of rationalization and cost-consciousness is blowing through the Swiss administrative system, reflected in a freeze on new recruitment and budget cuts. Here again, information is lacking with which to define the criteria on which reductions are based in the areas affected.

Existing machinery does not seem appropriate to cope with these new demands. And while lawyers and political analysts may have been the first to say so, the government is now taking up the baton.

The backdrop to the situation just described is a steady and regular withdrawal by electors from participation in public affairs, most markedly at the federal level. Some observers interpret this loss of public interest as a questioning of state activities. The issue then is the credibility and legitimacy of the public authorities. Given that, politicians may see evaluation as a way of demonstrating their determination to go further towards meeting the electorate's needs and of investing the interventions by public authorities with legitimate authority.

Which Way Forward
for Evaluation in Switzerland?

In the face of the as-yet hazy perception of this very slowly emerging new need, the Federal Department of Justice and Public Order assumed responsibility, after intervention by Parliament, for setting up a think tank of civil servants and outside experts on the need for, and conditions of, legislative evaluation. The group was set up in late 1987.

At the same time, a five-million-franc national research program was announced, to be run under the aegis of the Swiss National Research Fund, beginning in 1989. The aim will be to increase understanding of the methods of funding, of optimization, and of the effects of the various implementing instruments, and to address a major need felt by the official political and scientific bodies and administrative agencies. The research will be expected to provide answers to these questions. Should the objectives be fixed and should expected outcomes be legislated on or not? Is state intervention justified? What cases should be left to self-evaluation, placing reliance on the actors of economic and social life or market forces? (All these are taken from the national program.) This first real effort at scientific research into evaluation in Switzerland — where studies to date on public policies have centered chiefly on the decision-making and implementing processes (Linder 1987) — should result in cross-disciplinary studies conducted in close cooperation with practitioners, focusing on concrete problems.

While the group of experts in overall charge of the program has still to define the areas for analysis, central importance will nonetheless attach to determining what type of evaluative procedures will be most suited to the Swiss politico-administrative system, and in what conditions they should be applied to ensure that their findings are usable and used.

References

Aubert, J. F. 1967. *Traité de droit constitutionnel*. Vol. 1 et 2. Paris: Dalloz.

Bundesamfur, J. 1985. *Bericht der Arbeitsgruppe* "Gesetzevaluation." Bern: Eidg. Justiz- und Polizeidepartement.

Buschor, E. 1987. *Les buts et les limites du contrôle administratif*. Rapport de la Conférence annuelle de la Société Suisse des sciences administratives 7. Bern.

Delley, J. D. 1984. *La mise en oeuvre des politiques publiques in Manuel Système politique de la Suisse*. vol. 2. Bern-Stuttgart: Haupt.

Germann, R., and A. Fruttiger. 1981. *Ausserparlamentarische Kommissionen: die Milizverwaltung des Bundes*. Bern.

Jans, A. 1985. "Einige Bemerkungen zur Politikevaluation in der Schweiz." Paper for the European Group of Public Administration. Leuven, Belgien. 3–6 September.

Knapp, B. 1987. "La Confédération et les cantons; l'influence des crises sur l'évolution de leurs relations." *La Suisse, Pouvoirs* no. 43, Paris: PUF.

Kloti, U. 1987. *Regierungsprogramm und Entscheidungsprozess*. Bern-Stuttgart: Haupt.

Linder, W. 1987. *La décision politique en Suisse: Genèse et mise en oeuvre de la législation*. Lausanne: Réalites sociales.

Mader, L. 1985. *L'évaluation législative: Pour une analyse empirique des effets de la législation*. Lausanne: Payot.

Mastronardi, P. 1987. *Les commissions de gestion et le contrôle de l'impact de l'action étatique*. Lausanne: IDHEAP.

Morand, C.-A. 1987. "La formation et la mise en. oeuvre du droit." *La Suisse, Pouvoirs* no. 43, Paris: PUF.

Reszler, A. 1986. *Mythes et identité de la Suisse*. Genève: Georg.

Schmid, G. 1983. "Funktionen des Rechts im politischen System der Schweiz." in *Manuel Systéme politique de la Suisse* 1. Bern-Stuttgart: Haupt.

Urio, P. 1972. *L'affaire des Mirages: Décision administrative et contrôle parlementaire*. Genève: Médecine et Hygiène.

IV

Overview and Synthesis

9

Genesis and Structure of Evaluation Efforts in Comparative Perspective

Hans-Ulrich Derlien

Summarizing and comparing the various national reports presented in this volume is not an easy task to accomplish. The national development of evaluation depends on a number of factors and constellations. This context has historically grown and constitutes a part of national (and increasingly international) collective learning.

The conditions under which the evaluation function in the various countries developed are not merely interdependent, but they also influence the subsequent structure and operation of the evaluation systems that emerge. Nevertheless, for analytical purposes the complicated fabric first has to be unwoven into a summary which deals with the genesis, the historical process and sociopolitical roots of evaluation efforts. Part two will systematically treat individual change agents who played a role in the process of institutionalizing the evaluation function. Part three of the chapter will describe the elements which make up the present national evaluation systems (if there are such) and will try to outline the modes of their operation.

I should like to emphasize that this summary as a matter of course draws most of its information from the national reports included in this volume. Furthermore, I have tried to outline arguments presented during the meetings of the working group. To arrive at some coherent conceptualization, interpolations were necessary which were drawn from the relevant literature; thanks to the response of the working group members to the first draft I could eliminate most of the misconclusions and was in a position to fill in more accurate data.

Genesis of Evaluation Efforts

The overall impression one might derive from the reports is that policy evaluation has reached different developmental stages and degrees of maturity. This is so, both in terms of length of experience with this analytical tool to improve public policy by systematic learning from past performance of programs, and in terms of frequency, regularity, and ultimately degree of institutionalization of the evaluation function.

At present I would tentatively classify the state of the art in the countries surveyed here as follows:

- Undoubtedly the most advanced evaluation system can be observed in the United States. Looking back on roughly twenty years of experience with policy evaluation since the 1960s, the American system has reached a high degree of methodological sophistication. This development allows one to clearly distinguish PE from other more traditional techniques of accounting and auditing. In addition, the U.S. evaluation system is firmly institutionalized within the bureaucracy and within the legislative branch (including the General Accounting Office (GAO)) and consequently produces a huge number of studies. Furthermore, the American system seems to have affected the philosophy, the skills, and the willingness of other countries to introduce policy evaluation, too.
- With the first examples of policy evaluation reaching back into the 1960s, Sweden, Canada, and the Federal Republic of Germany (FRG) may be distinguished as a second group of countries following the U.S. efforts relatively early. However, despite institutionalization of PE in various policy areas, their systems remained rather fragmented and the number of studies carried out seems to be relatively low.
- Great Britain and Canada both, apparently, have reemphasized PE at the end of the 1970s after earlier attempts at planning and evaluation had been regarded as unsuccessful. The two countries, however, have institutionalized the evaluation function in different ways. While Canada attributed evaluation to a Comptroller General as well as to individual government departments, in Great Britain evaluation hardly seems to have an organizational locus, but rather appears to be part of the general management philosophy.
- It would also be possible to put Great Britain together with Norway, Denmark, France, Switzerland, and the Netherlands — those countries which in the 1980s have emphasized policy evaluation beyond ad hoc studies in an effort to increase productivity in government. Some of them have linked policy evaluation closely to the budget process.

In the following sections, the history of the various national evaluation efforts is to be more closely inspected, and some contextual factors are elaborated which may well have influenced the propensity of the various national systems to move towards policy evaluation.

Historical Account of Institutionalization

The roots of the U.S. evaluation efforts traditionally are seen in President Johnson's War on Poverty programs of the mid-1960s and the concomitant efforts to rationalize policy making by institutionalizing the famous planning programming budgeting system (PPBS) in 1965. It is worthwhile keeping in mind this connection between intervention policy and PPBS on the one hand and evaluation on the other. While the federal departments, above all the Office of Economic Opportunity, created evaluation staffs to monitor the results of their welfare programs, the U.S. Congress, not wanting to rely exclusively on executive branch studies, required in the Economic Opportunity Act of 1967 the General Accounting Office to assess the effectiveness of the poverty programs. Under the conservative Nixon administration, attempts were made to strengthen the evaluation function at the federal level by assigning to the Bureau of the Budget (BOB)[1] the task of stimulating departmental evaluation studies and fostering the spread of methodological know-how. Since then both these branches of U.S. government, the executive branch and Congress, have continuously increased their efforts to make evaluation a regular procedure. Despite the 1979 Office of Management and Budget (OMB) circular A-117 renewing the request for evaluations, legislative efforts seem to have contributed more to the persistence of PE in the U.S. system, be it the introduction of Sunset Legislation (Adams and Sherman 1978), or the institutionalization of the Institute for Program Evaluation in the GAO in 1980, with nearly one hundred professional staff (later renamed Program Evaluation and Methodology Division). These capacities, along with other congressional analytic capacities, are the more important in recent years, as the executive branch departments have dramatically reduced their evaluation units since 1980.

In the FRG, too, the emergence of PE is closely connected with intensifying social and economic interventions and reform policies under the government led by a Social-Democrat chancellor in 1969. The landscape, however, is much more fragmented, and evaluation has not been as firmly institutionalized as in the United States. Some departments have created evaluation sections, while others have their programs evaluated under the cover of general research activities commissioned to outside contractors. Most characteristic for the early 1970s was a number of experiments (basically in education) which, however, did not reach the level of methodological sophistication of the large-scale U.S. experiments (Rossi and Wright 1977).

Apart from these program-specific institutionalizations, PE became institutionalized in the budget process in 1973 and thus enables the Finance Ministry to request studies from individual departments. This, however, has seldom been done. An equally weak position has a methods section in the Chancellor's Office, which does not even stimulate the departments to carry out evaluations, nor does it assist them in their evaluation attempts.

Although the necessity to evaluate programs has been emphasized as a logical consequence of the planning cycle and the concept is generally accepted, an evaluation culture has not yet developed. This may be due to the somewhat ambivalent role the German federal Parliament plays in this regard: on the one hand there are occasional requests for evaluation studies and legislated evaluation demands; on the other hand one has to state a lack of discussion of the roughly two hundred annual reports (including evaluations) which Parliament receives. The scientific staff of the Bundestag is too small and lacks policy analysts. Neither has the German Federal Audit Office played an active role in enforcing an evaluation system on the executive branch, nor has it carried out systematic studies itself; recently, however, evaluation has been acknowledged as a task of the GAO in principle.

Like the German government, the socialist Swedish government, too, was preoccupied with launching and expanding programs until the mid-1970s, while relying for oversight on traditional accounting and financial reviews. Although recognized in theory as a necessary part of the new planning, programming, and budgeting–influenced administrative systems, policy evaluation was much less important than planning, programming, and budgeting. In contrast to the FRG, the reforms relied on a broad political consensus typical for Sweden, and the programs were based on extensive ex ante analysis in committees including social scientists. PPBS, as a concept, has had a greater bearing in Sweden than in the FRG. Not surprisingly, then, effectiveness auditing and program-cost accounting were introduced as early as the mid-1960s. In the central government this development was inspired and implemented by the National Audit Bureau (Ysander 1983, 10). A great portion of its audits are policy evaluation carried out by some one hundred academics trained in economics, social science, and business administration. In view of economic stagnation a period of broad reappraisal of existing policies started at the end of the 1970s. Both Social-Democrat and nonSocialist (1976–82) governments have emphasized the need for more thorough appraisal of policies and programs. Evaluation units have been established within supervising national agencies. In addition, expert groups attached to ministries have redirected some of their interest from planning to evaluation. Still, however, policy evaluation cannot be considered as institutionalized in the ministerial work or in Parliament.

The reappraisal of policies rather than of programs seems to have been also the task of the British Program Analysis and Review (PAR), coordinated by the Central Policy Review Staff (CPRS, 1970), and the Treasury. This central PAR, however, faded by the mid-1970s without recognizably putting its stamp on departmental-review activities. Despite formally abolishing PAR in 1979 and CPRS in 1983, it was the conservative Thatcher government that reactivated the early evaluation impulse in its emphasis on "value for money" and in its managerialist policy approach. While the 1983 Financial Management Initiative concentrated on inputs, nevertheless, prospectively new policies were required to make provision for subsequent evaluation. Further, in 1985 a Joint Management Unit was created with the aim of making evaluation a regular activity of the departments.

The recent efforts of the British government have been accompanied by increased parliamentary emphasis on evaluation and by strengthening the Public Accounts Committee (PAC). For example, the National Audit Office established in 1983 was not only to replace the Exchequer and Audit Department, but also to serve the PAC. It remains to be seen if this new system really arrives at evaluation or merely effectuates traditional accounting procedures.

Historically and systematically Canada probably comes closest to the constellation under which policy evaluation became institutionalized in the United States. Not only did Canada adopt the PPBS in 1969 (and retained it), but also the Treasury Board set up a Planning Branch, which developed evaluation capacity and support for departmental evaluation efforts. Nevertheless, by the 1980s policy evaluation turned out to have been largely unsuccessful in Canadian central government. Again, it was the legislative branch, in this instance the Canadian Parliament, which in 1977 with the help of the Auditor General pressed the government to create the Office of Comptroller General. This office contained a special Program Evaluation Branch to promote policy evaluation as part of the management cycle.

An interesting Canadian feature is the resulting impetus of these parliamentary initiatives to institutionalize policy evaluation with the permanent deputy head of departments and to create evaluation units in each department. At the same time policy evaluation within the Policy and Expenditure Management System (introduced in 1979) is related to the executive budget process through the Treasury Board's requirements to submit evaluation results and evaluation plans. It is indicative of the degree of institutionalization that in Canada (as well as in the United States) government manuals exist, which prescribe the formal properties and the methodology of evaluation studies.

While the United States, Sweden, and the FRG have continued their early evaluation efforts into the 1980s (although with different degrees of institutionalization and frequency of studies), and while Canada and Great Britain have taken a second attempt in the late 1970s, there is a third group of countries where the use of evaluation studies was limited (Netherlands) or almost absent (Denmark, Norway) until quite recently.

In the Netherlands a government reform commission in 1980 and, more recently, Parliament pressed for evaluation as a regular policy-making device, after earlier attempts by the Finance Ministry to promote programming and policy analysis had failed. The Center-Liberal government in 1981 took initiative to procedurally institutionalize policy evaluation with the annual budget process (Reconsiderations Procedure). As in Britain, the driving force behind policy evaluation is the government's aim to roll back the frontier of the state and to reverse a long political tradition of social-intervention policy.

The philosophical link to Britain is even more obvious in the Norwegian case, where evaluation was institutionalized in 1985 as part of the reforms in the government budgetary system, following a productivity campaign in 1982. Furthermore, in Norway the auditor general, who reports exclusively to the legislature, has adopted performance auditing in addition to traditional financial auditing — almost twenty years later than Sweden, whose administrative innovations are normally readily introduced in Norway.

Finally, in some countries, such as Denmark, the concept of evaluation has spread in the 1980s. Evaluation studies are mainly undertaken by research institutes, although the device is not formally institutionalized in national government. In addition, since 1973 the Danish Department of Administration and Reorganization, together with the Ministry of Finance, has regularly evaluated various policy areas. France serves as an example of a country which relies heavily on traditional legal and accounting control instruments. Only in 1982 (under the Socialist presidency) was evaluation stressed as a necessity. In 1983, a survey of the audit and research reports produced so far was undertaken in order to find out the extent to which they have evaluative contents (Quermonne and Rouban 1986). Switzerland at best seems to feel the need for PE at present; this case will serve us for discussing factors which could have inhibited the development of policy evaluation.

This rough outline of the development of PE in the various countries reveals three trends:

- In the 1980s there emerges a second movement concerned with questions of output and, to a lesser extent, impact. Even most of those countries that institutionalized evaluation at the end of the 1960s experienced a second shift of evaluation activities.
- While the first evaluation movement of the 1960s and 1970s was closely linked to the planning and programming process and thus to the role of the program administrator, the attempts of the late 1970s and the 1980s are, rather, geared to either the political level, reconsidering the justification of policies, or to the budgetary process. In both cases the role of the external auditors became important.
- The locus of evaluation consequently has shifted in the 1980s from being primarily an internal government operation to becoming a concern of parliaments. Concomitantly, the actors have changed, too. Now one finds the Parliament as a key center of activity along with those auditing offices that primarily report to Parliament and have, therefore, been brought into the game.

We may ask now, which factors determined the variation in maturity of the evaluation systems and which constellations were influential in the observed individual developmental patterns. In the following section, I shall discuss exogenous factors responsible for the state of the art, as well as those endogenous factors, that is, characteristics of the internal environment of national government, which can be isolated as change agents.

Fiscal Situation

The distinct developmental patterns of the early starters — the United States, Sweden, Canada, and the FRG — from most of the other countries following along at the end of the 1970s or later, might be related among other factors to the conditions of the national economies and thus to the fiscal situation of the respective governments.

The first group of countries got the impulse for PE during the 1960s, that is, a time of booming economies and growing budgets, which enabled governments to embark on expensive social intervention programs including education and health care. In this context formal planning systems emerged, which either were limited to medium-term financial planning (FRG) or even attempted to integrate budgeting with programming (the United States, Sweden, Canada). In any case, evaluation was either regarded logically as part of these planning systems or as necessitated by the information needs of the intervention programs, the results of which could hardly be predicted with a sufficient degree of certainty. Evaluations, then, were primarily used by program managers to effectuate existing and new programs. Only occasionally were evaluations necessary to protect these programs against political opponents by proving their effectiveness.

The impact of the totally different economic situation of the late 1970s on evaluation was almost the same: shrinking economies and the necessity to manage scarcity induced stress on governments and led to the development of cutback management techniques (Schick 1988). The way by which the relatively unfavorable economic and the critical fiscal situation promoted evaluation was via the budget process: financial management initiatives (Great Britain, Canada, Norway, the Netherlands) either made use of previous evaluation efforts (Canada, Great Britain) and thus engendered a second wave of evaluation efforts, or the new managerialism introduced the concept of evaluation in order to rationalize resource allocation within the budget (Norway, the Netherlands). Typically, the bearers of this second evaluation movement are not the program administrators in the government departments, but rather the finance ministers and the auditing offices as the traditional wardens of the budget. Consequently, the perspective on and the function of evaluation slightly shifted: instead of effectuating programs, the emphasis was rather on curbing ineffective programs in order to cut back the national budget.

Political Constellation

Of course, it is not the economic situation per se which brings about changes in policy direction, but ultimately politicians and government parties change the course of the ship of state. In the booming 1960s the countries of the first evaluation wave were governed by reformist parties (Social-Democrats in the FRG and Sweden, Democrats in the United States, Liberals in Canada) who engaged in the various reform policies and had a clear affinity to the employment of social-science methods needed for policy evaluation. Another case in point might be the Socialist presidency in France (1981), which put an emphasis on evaluation in 1982.

Rather conservative governments (the United States 1968–74, 1979–present; Great Britain 1970–1974, 1979–present; Canada 1979, 1984–present; Norway 1981–86; Denmark since 1982; Sweden 1976–82; Netherlands 1977–81, 1982–present), often facing a less prosperous economic situation, made use of existing evaluation instruments not only to retailor the budget, but occasionally in an attempt to curb reform programs of their predecessor governments, which they had viewed with suspicion from the beginning. This is not to mean that interventionist political parties, were they in a position to govern, would not have had to respond to the changed economic situation in a similar way. In addition, conservative governments tend to look at social scientists with suspicion or to feel that they are the advocates of the former reform policies; their enlightening function is regarded skeptically. On the other hand, where analytical capacities were firmly established, incoming conservative administrations could try to use them as means of "analytical delegitimation" (Wagner and Wollmann 1986a).

Not surprisingly, there is also a neoconservative international consensus that the state should withdraw from society or should at least not further expand, and that many a program had overshot its goal. In connection with policies of privatization, deregulation and de-bureaucratization, scrapping the planning system, which had served to develop reform programs, was one device to change the course (United States 1970; FRG 1982; Great Britain 1979; Denmark 1983). The other was to improve the traditional budgetary track by importing accounting techniques from the private sector — techniques that had to deal with output (less with impact) of programs as the unit of analysis and that therefore resembled evaluation methods. After all, modernized accounting techniques fitted the traditional auditing procedures of the audit offices.

Constitutional Features

An explanation of the distinctive developmental paths followed by the various national systems that concentrated solely on the correlation between expanding economy/intervention programs/social-democrat governments or shrinking economy/austerity policy/conservative governments would be too simple a model (Wagner and Wollmann 1986a). It would, for instance, not explain the change in the United States starting under the Republican Nixon administration as early as 1970, nor would it explain why almost nothing changed after a conservative government had taken power in Bonn in 1982. Of prime importance seems to be the constitutional relationship between the executive and the legislative branches of government as an additional variable.

In parliamentary party government systems the classical theory of division of power hardly holds true empirically; here the cabinet has a strong hold on the parliamentary majority or shares the interests and programmatic consensus of the majority faction(s), while it is merely the opposition faction(s) who have a strong motivation to control the executive, but who regularly are not in a position to enforce controls on it. The short historical account presented earlier has shed light on the propagating role of parliaments in systems of party government (Canada, Norway, Britain). It might, however, be supposed that parliaments merely emphasized what the administration wanted anyway. The German experience of an active parliamentary role with respect to the institutionalization of evaluation in 1968–1969 is a case in point: during this period a grand coalition was in government. In general, however, there are no visible differences between the political parties as far as policy evaluation is concerned.

The situation might be completely different in presidential government systems like those of the United States and France, where parliamentary majorities may form against a president and enforce measures on an administration in order to enhance their control capacity or informational independence. What wonder that a powerful U.S. Congress built up a huge congressional staff and made use of this counterbureaucracy to check the program administrators in the executive branch? In such a setting the legislative branch becomes a strong pillar in the evaluation system even when evaluation efforts originated in the administration. Legislative interest might help to keep executive evaluation capacities in place, even if the administration is not too enthusiastic about it, because the administration then needs these analytic staffs to keep the informational balance of power vis-à-vis Congress. France deviates from this configuration, because Parliament is constitutionally weaker and the executive branch is rather self-sufficient in its orientation towards using social-science policy advice in general (Wagner and Wollmann, 1986b).

Another constitutional factor which could be of importance in this respect is the affiliation of the central accounting or auditing unit. In most countries these offices are regarded as assisting units of the legislative branch and report to parliament (United States, Canada, Norway, the Netherlands, Denmark). The GAO in the FRG has historically been attached to the executive branch, and only since 1969 has it slightly redirected its function also to serve Parliament and the small parliamentary audit committee. Similarly, the French Cours des Comptes, although reporting to Parliament, too, has an executive bias owing to the career patterns of its members (Nioche and Poinsard 1985). In Sweden with its tradition of small ministries and highly independent agencies, the dominant audit institution, the National Audit Bureau, is exclusively an instrument of the central government. Its reports are either directed to the audited agency or to the government when principle matters are brought up. The parliamentary auditors here have a small staff to undertake ad hoc scrutinies.

The more a central auditing unit is independent of the executive branch and even attached to parliament, the more parliament may be tempted to use these institutions as a power basis and a source of counteradvice vis-à-vis even a party government. In the American case this arrangement, of course, could but strengthen congressional evaluation efforts.

Supply of Social-Science Knowledge

Evaluation methods and policy analysis in general have nowhere been invented by the bureaucracy, but have been developing in the realm of the social sciences and economics. There are strong indications that the developmental stage of the respective government evaluation culture is decisively dependent on the propensity of the academic world to produce evaluation devices, engage in evaluations, and professionalize the roles of evaluators and policy analysts in general (Wagner and Wollmann 1986b).

Undoubtedly, the leading role of the United States in institutionalizing evaluation procedures and in creating evaluation staffs in government to a great deal also reflects the long tradition of applied (quantitative) social research. This supply seems not to be readily available in most of the other countries. In these countries there is either no tradition of applied social-science research in universities, or the professionalization of the social sciences (curricula, scientific associations, specific jobs) has only started in the 1970s.

These diverging antecedent conditions also could have indirectly affected the receptivity of the administration for the diffusion of evaluation skills, as they determine the probability that social scientists or economists are recruited at least into bureaucratic staff positions. This was the case in the United States and Canada and, to a lesser extent, in the FRG and Great Britain (Bulmer 1988). The Swedish case is indicative, too: in the 1960s economics, business, and public administration graduates reached leading positions in the public sector and were also the only recruits of the National Audit Bureau, when it started effectiveness auditing.

If the bureaucracy (and politicians in the legislative branch) have overwhelmingly undergone a training in law (France, Germany, Denmark) or even classics (Great Britain), the system might be less receptive for social scientists and social-science knowledge.

Furthermore the existence of independent, non-university research institutes providing evaluation capacities seems to depend on a strong tradition of applied social sciences. In a number of countries new policy-research institutes were founded in the 1970s (see the subsection "Internal versus External Evaluation Research" in this chapter).

Clearly, these factors explain differences in the supply of evaluation studies, and by way of staff affinity to the social sciences also affect the demand for this kind of information. A lack of scientific infrastructure would also aggravate the institutionalization of policy evaluation even when the need for this kind of analysis arises.

Functional Equivalents

It is equally interesting, however, to ask which conditions — ceteris paribus — explain the lack of demand for evaluation research. Among other factors, it might be the availability of functionally equivalent kinds of information, in particular good official statistics. One could possibly maintain that in continental Europe and Scandinavia, that is, in countries with a long (and still strong) state tradition, the statistical apparatus is one of the backbones of the bureaucracy on which policy analysts (and economists) customarily rely. A case in point could be the Netherlands with their long planning tradition originating in Tinbergen's efforts. On the other hand, historically it was the very absence of a reliable statistical apparatus which gave rise to applied social science in the United States.

Second, apart from the census system, internal administrative data (process-produced information) are possibly not evenly available in all of the countries under investigation.

Another equivalent, which for quite a long time seems to have satisfied the rising evaluative-information demand in all of the countries, is the existence of an advisory committee system around central government. This feature was reported for Sweden, where almost all reforms were developed and reassessed by ad hoc committees; for Denmark; and for the Netherlands. Policies are here assessed by experts from science, interest groups, and bureaucratic professions; this system could at least offer what project managers are not seldom most interested in: implementation assessments.

Last but not least, some evaluative information, which indicates the need for program amendment, is produced by the system of administrative courts in countries with a strong public-law tradition or by the ombudsman (Denmark, Sweden, Norway, the Netherlands). Investigative journalism seems to play an important role in countries that disclose documents under freedom of information acts (the United States, Sweden, Canada).

Retarding Factors

Of course, all of the countries under scrutiny have accepted by now the need and the notion of policy evaluation. In trying to sort out factors that could explain the different developmental stages the various countries have reached, we should also mention some of the factors which possibly contributed to a slow or late development of policy evaluation.

The above-mentioned functional equivalents surely might have retarded the introduction of policy evaluation. As far as features of the old continental state apparatus were concerned (official statistics, administrative courts), these point to the public-law tradition as a more general condition. Recruitment of jurists into the political (to a lesser extent) and bureaucratic (France, Germany, Denmark) elite shapes the role understanding of actors in all subsystems, parliament, administration, and auditing offices in a peculiar way: questions relating to efficiency and effectiveness are at best asked in the second instance; to think in terms of programs (with stated goals and projects to achieve them) is rather alien to people who are used to consider laws in principle as made for eternity, although practically laws are frequently amended and increasingly aim at specific effects to be achieved. Furthermore, the external control apparatus (administrative courts, auditing offices) primarily investigates the legality of decisions and actions, thus moving the focus away from the effectiveness of programs. In such a politico-administrative culture, the idea of policy evaluation is more likely to find reception and propagation in the realms of social science and economics, and its extension depends on these professions finding their way into core institutions.

We also considered whether the federal or unitary constitution of a state had an effect on the extent to which PE was applied. Have the centers of federations a higher need to monitor implementation? It would be plausible to assume such an information need where programs are executed by offices of member states (FRG, Canada), but less where the central government executes programs through its own field offices (United States). Thus, in Canada and the FRG, where joint federal-state programs on a shared-cost basis were launched, evaluations were institutionalized to make sure that programs met national standards. It is indicative that the Swiss federal government in 1987 institutionalized a think tank to explore evaluation possibilities.

Monitoring is more easily accomplished in unitary states where the center can request the field offices to provide statistics. In a federal system with administrative autonomy of the members, however, it is occasionally not feasible, at least politically, to demand detailed information from the states, unless the procurement is especially institutionalized.

Another variable of potential importance could be the extent to which government programs and services are delivered by nongovernmental organizations, be it by commercial organizations or by commonweal, nonprofit organizations. Here in principle the argument raised above (federalism) would hold true as well. A new constellation, though, emerges when services, which elsewhere derive from government programs, are provided completely privately, that is, under societal self-regulation and self-help. Obviously, here the volume of state intervention and activity would be rather small, at least in particular policy areas, and the need to monitor effects of government policies would be minor (although in rationalist perspective the demand for social indicators and societal monitoring would increase). This argument can be related to federalism again: of course, central government's information needs decisively depend on the division of jurisdictions between center and subsystems; where, as in Switzerland, the federal government has centralized only few competences, we would not expect much policy evaluation. Would the need for PE then be felt the stronger on the subgovernmental level?

This line of reasoning leads us to another factor of potential importance: the size of a country and administrative distance. Smaller countries (in terms of territory, population, or both) might have smaller problems with less local variation and less need for central intervention in many policy areas. This hypothesis, however, does not hold true in the cases of Denmark and Sweden with their large public sectors. If in addition to small size the political system is decentralized (Switzerland), or the administration is de-concentrated onto the local level (Denmark), the administrative distance between the population/problems and the regulating authority is small, and feedback from society reaches the steering bodies and political institutions more directly. In the most extreme case where there are few general societal problems and many locally confined problem areas dealt with by autonomous local government units, the impact of measures could be directly inspected, cause and effect could easily be related to one another, and PE as an artificial feedback mechanism would be regarded as superfluous. However, with central government programs operating in such a decentralized structure, the need for central evaluation seems to increase, if uniformity with national goals is regarded as necessary.

Obviously, it is hardly possible to attribute the developmental stage of PE exclusively to one of the factors mentioned above. After all, the search for an explanation of the observed differences should not distract our attention from a very common phenomenon: changes in the repertoire of tools for managing public affairs are heavily subject to fashions and fads. Administrative philosophies (in particular planning systems and management styles) come and go like tides. New ideas are often introduced from private management (Sweden in the 1960s) and are then transferred from one government to the other, not merely because they have proven useful, but also because governments want to be thought of as modern and to view themselves as innovative. Cross-fertilization was reported for Scandinavia, where Sweden plays a leading role, and for North America, with the United States having provided the example for planning and evaluation. In general, the spillover of concepts is facilitated where countries formally cooperate and specialists gather in international associations like, for instance, the supreme audit institutions (INTOSAI).

Once a reform has been carried through, the new management structures press for consistent control mechanisms. A case in point can be observed not only in the evolution of evaluation from formal planning systems, but also after the introduction of management by objectives and decentralized budget spending in Sweden: both measures increased the need for evaluative information to keep the management system operating.

It might be justified to summarize the historical process leading to the institutionalization of PE in a two-stage model. While a first wave of evaluations in the 1960s was closely linked to social-reform policies of social-liberal governments operating under favorable fiscal conditions, a second wave of the evaluation movement was stimulated by predominantly, although not exclusively, conservative governments' attempts to curb intervention programs in view of fiscal strains. Consequently, there is a tendency to reorient PE from its predominant focus on programs and their improvement towards the budget and its curtailment. A concomitant shift of the central actors can be observed, too: instead of departmental program managers, finance and audit institutions, in particular those serving functions for national parliament, become protagonists of policy evaluation.

This picture by no means holds true for all countries surveyed. There are quite a number of continental European countries where a variety of constitutional, administrative, and cultural factors have hampered the process of institutionalizing PE as a regular activity in the politico-administrative system. Nevertheless, even in these countries the demand for (ad hoc) evaluations seems to have increased in response to the general political and economic forces operating in the early 1980s.

Change Agents

Once the demand for evaluative information is perceived and acknowledged in a polity, it is nevertheless still far from being satisfied. It is almost an anthropological proposition that people do not like to be supervised and resist having their activities monitored, because they basically fear negative sanctions in general and threats to their careers in particular resulting from the documentation of failures. In addition, external controls — by definition — change the existing balance of power between organizational systems and therefore are resisted for political reasons. It is also frequently the case that resistance arises not only when new control measures are being introduced, but is already arising when concepts are discussed. Therefore it is worthwhile to look at the agents which brought about change, even in the face of resistance from other parts of the national polity.

Parliament

National parliaments have been pressing their executive branches to introduce policy evaluation. In the FRG the legislative branch demanded evaluation studies in the fields of developmental aid and technology policy in the late 1960s, but did not specialize internally for this function, nor did the Parliament establish specialized staff capacity. In Canada, Parliament took up the initiative of the auditor general in 1977 and entitled him to supervise executive evaluation efforts. In Britain, too, Parliament since 1979 strengthened the system of select committees. These initiatives always addressed the executive to produce evaluations. In the United States the role of Congress for constitutional reasons was more powerful: apart from legislating evaluation requirements in laws (as did parliaments in other countries, too) and introducing sunset legislation, Congress, with the help of the GAO and other staffs, built up its own evaluation capacities to conduct its oversight responsibilities vis-à-vis the executive branch.

In other countries (the Netherlands, Norway) parliaments have changed their budgeting procedures and put more emphasis on evaluation in full consent with governments.

Supreme Auditing Institutions

In most of the countries, in particular in those which followed on the second wave of the evaluation movement, the auditing offices played an active role. In Sweden performance auditing, of which policy evaluation is an integral part, became the core function of the National Audit Bureau (NAB) as early as 1967, while financial auditing (until 1987) had been moved to local offices. Furthermore, the NAB promotes evaluation by issuing guidelines and offering seminars. In the United States the GAO established its evaluation office in 1980; in Canada the auditor general pointed to a need to improve the policy evaluation function since 1976 and induced Parliament to institutionalize his role in this respect more explicitly. A similar development took place in Britain, where the Exchequer and Audit Department was replaced by the National Audit Office in 1983. In Denmark cost accounting was emphasized by the national auditors in 1985. In the Dutch and German cases the GAOs have rather played a reactive role. Although they are entitled to review all government operations with respect to efficiency and effectiveness and to assess evaluation procurements in their executive branches, their traditional role of checking conformity with budget law and controlling formal correctness of operations, which they have in common with all accounting offices, seems to be still dominant. Nevertheless, their role understanding is changing in response to growing concerns about efficiency and effectiveness in other parts of the national policy. The Dutch GAO has produced a number of reports on large projects. The German Bundesrechnungshof in 1985 has finally explicitly accepted the evaluation function as part of its broad supervisory role and even carried out a survey of the state of the art in federal departments in 1986. To date this survey has not been published.

The Cabinet

Has evaluation been a concern of cabinets; that is, have there been central political initiatives in the executive branch? Either the findings in this respect are in inverse proportion to the rather active role parliaments and auditing offices have played, or cabinet initiatives were complementary. Some cabinets took broad political initiatives to increase productivity in general: for example, the Netherlands' Reconsiderations Procedure in 1981, Norway's 1982 Productivity Campaign, Britain's 1983 Financial Management Initiative, and Canada's 1979 Policy and Expenditure Management System. In Sweden, the government's leading policy has been to convince agencies to evaluate their programs, increase their effectiveness, facilitate adaptions to across-the-board cutbacks, or all three. These cases belong to the second wave stimulated by unfavorable economic developments and their governments' concern to manage the state budget more efficiently and to limit its further growth. That the early starters in the 1960s lacked central policy initiatives to establish evaluation capacities is plausible, because their administrations' concern was with developing reform policies. While evaluation in those days might have appeared to be a nonpolitical technical device, in the 1980s managing the budget has become an issue of political priority and therefore has attracted the cabinets' attention and paved the way for evaluation techniques.

Central Government Units

This is not to say that only recently would one find central units in national government dealing with evaluation. The U.S. OMB had taken on the role of advising the departments to conduct evaluation studies as early as 1970, and it reemphasized this concern in 1979. In Britain, too, the Central Policy Review Staff within the PAR procedure had tried to motivate departments to undertake studies, as has Rayner's Efficiency Unit since 1979. In the Netherlands attempts had been made to strengthen policy analysis in general by establishing the interdepartmental Committee for the Development of Policy Analysis in the 1970s and, as its successor in 1985, the Agency for Policy Analysis under the purview of the Ministry of Finance. Canada is the outstanding example of a recent creation of a special central office concerned with evaluation: the Office of Comptroller General, created in 1978. Here the mandate of the office is to function as a change agent towards more evaluation in the departments.

One probably may generalize that, where central units exist, they took on the task of promoting evaluations throughout government, to develop guidelines and give assistance to departments. Their role is nowhere to evaluate departmental programs themselves. Obviously, it has been recognized in all of the countries that such an interference with (partly formal) departmental autonomy would have seriously driven up the level of conflict in (coalition) governments.

When regarding central government units one should also take into account the department or office which centrally controls the executive budget cycle. The organizational position of the U.S. OMB as an office of the White House is outstanding and has enabled it to exert authority in promoting evaluations. Apart from this authority derived from its formal position, the degree to which evaluation results are linked to next year's budget seems to be of prime importance for the success of this central solution. Normal finance ministries can acquire the same influence over departmental evaluation activities, once the latter are related to the budget process (and thus sanctioned and reinforced). For instance, the Dutch Ministry of Finance has its hands in the intradepartmental study groups which prepare reports for the Reconsiderations Procedure. One reason why the Finance Ministry in the FRG has hardly influenced the departments despite its formal right to request studies is the fact that it has seldom used this authority and, thus, never integrated evaluation with budgeting. The Danish rotating evaluation system performed by the Department of Administration and Reorganization annually selects critical issues from varying policy areas for evaluation, but tends to be a consultant to the departments rather than a budget controller. The Swedish Ministry of Finance established an independent expert group in 1981, which—inter alia—produces ad hoc evaluations in all policy areas, and the Dutch Ministry of Finance is assisted by an Agency for Policy Analysis.

It seems to be the advantage of the recent neoconservative managerialist over the previous program orientation of evaluation to establish precisely this link between evaluation and budgeting. It remains to be seen, however, what effects this may have on the substance of evaluations. One potentially negative outcome could be a decrease in the level of methodological sophistication. Another could be that the budgeting process will be confronted with biased success stories and not objective data as justifications for additional funds.

Departments

It is hardly possible to generalize about the role the departments have played in bringing about policy evaluation. Clearly central political initiatives or external pressures were needed in many cases to move them towards evaluation. On the other hand, there have always been some departments that started evaluations on their own initiative. Take, for instance, the then U.S. Office of Economic Opportunity or, in many countries, those departments involved in developmental aid. In these instances it was the information requirements of the programs, a number of social scientists among the personnel, and a minister committed to one program and its improvement or international practice stimulated by the United Nations or the World Bank that led to the establishment of evaluation staffs and to the commissioning of evaluation studies. Again, the recent Canadian move to make the deputy ministers responsible for departmental evaluations is unusual and reflects the central political initiative behind it. The normal case is probably that departments simply have programs or projects investigated as part of their ongoing normal research activities and that, for such efforts, they do not even term these studies "evaluations".

Where the quantity of these studies grew, departments were inclined to institute evaluation staffs or methodology sections in general. Frequently behind such a development stood the external pressures by parliament or the finance minister to produce a report (of any quality whatsoever) or to submit a cost-benefit analysis (as in the FRG).

As to the policy areas in which PE came to be practiced relatively early and which are being carried out most often today, it is probably not an overgeneralization to name developmental aid, labor market policy, health, and education. These were also the most common target areas of reformist policies.

The predominance of decentralized evaluation activities in the early developmental years also poses a methodological problem for writing a report like this. It is difficult to discover a system and, unless by some chance there have been observers in the field, in retrospect these early efforts may escape from our attention in view of more recent and spectacular central and systematic innovations. If longitudinal data on the number of accomplished studies were available, we could assess the decentralized activities more accurately; the availability of this type of statistics, however, would presuppose the very existence of a powerful evaluation movement.

Structure of Evaluation Arrangements

In this last section an attempt will be made to complement the genetic perspective by a systematic account of the evaluation arrangements devised in the various countries. The approach followed here will be procedurally oriented regarding evaluation as a process with distinct steps. The structural factors which have been analyzed above will be referred to, but will not constitute the core of the analysis. Thus, only those aspects of the activities of a specific institution, for instance the supreme auditor, which are relevant for understanding the evaluation process will be mentioned.

Initiation of Evaluations

Unless conducting evaluation studies becomes institutionalized, their occurrence tends to be random. Furthermore, the number of potential stimuli for studies is abundant, ranging from public criticism of a program, to spare research funds (which have to be spent before the end of the fiscal year), to a genuine need for the program administrator to know how the program worked out in practice. The following remarks will be confined to those initiatives which occur because the evaluation function is institutionalized somewhere in the politico-administrative system.

Legal obligation and parliamentary request Due to the outstanding role parliaments played in bringing about regular evaluations in most of the countries, it is not unusual for the imperative to carry out an evaluation to be laid down in the specific law or grant that authorizes the respective program. Examples of this kind of program-specific institutionalization and initiation include

- Economic Opportunity Act (United States, 1964)
- Compensatory Education Program (United States, 1965)
- Joint Federal-State Program of Regional Developmental Subsidies (FRG, 1969)
- Further Training Program in the Labor Market Law (FRG, 1969)
- Law of Continued Wage Payment in Case of Illness (FRG, 1969)

- Experimental Cash Public Assistance Program (DK, 1984)
- Law of Education and Training Allowance for Young Long-Term Unemployed Persons (DK, 1985)

In these mandated cases, the executive branch is obliged to produce a report to parliament after a certain period or at regular intervals; while the law is not always specific about the contents of the report, the task has been generally interpreted to mean evaluations. The practice of institutionalizing the evaluation in the authorizing legislation itself has been done in the United States by way of turning to sunset legislation as a general congressional policy. With this policy strategy, programs which have not proven effective in an evaluation expire automatically after a specific number of years. German Parliament has followed this device in a limited number of cases, although there is no juridical consensus yet whether a legislated program may be terminated at all.

Another mode in which parliaments become initiators of PE is the simple request for a periodic report from the executive branch. For instance, most of the two hundred regular executive-branch reports in the FRG (far from all of which are evaluations) to Parliament originate in standing parliamentary requests.

As evaluation studies almost always involve collecting and analyzing huge amounts of data, parliaments regularly ask the government bureaucracy to do the investigation, and often enough the actual research is further delegated to outside specialists (see the subsection "Internal versus External Evaluation Research" in this chapter). There is, however, an exception to the rule: where a parliament itself supports a large research staff and assistant offices, the initiatives will be more often directed towards these specialists in the legislative branch, as is the case in the United States. In these circumstances there are possible instances of parallel evaluations carried out in the executive branch as well as in these legislative support offices.

Initiatives of supreme audit institutions The national reports are not clear as to the extent the audit offices, which have been of paramount importance in institutionalizing evaluation, initiate and carry out evaluations themselves. Undoubtedly, the more the audit office has been the promoter of general evaluation activities in the executive branch, the more it will advise government and departments later on to evaluate specific measures, unless the department wants to evoke public criticism of the audit office. On the other hand, in the actual auditing process, evaluation studies are possibly carried out by the auditors themselves, depending on their expertise in this task. Both functions, advising the government to evaluate activities and carrying out studies of its own, are fulfilled by the U.S. GAO with its methodology division. Across all divisions and responsibilities, the GAO conducts approximately 1,050 studies at any one time.

It is important to stress that only a small number of these studies should be considered evaluations. Financial audits, management studies, and investigations of fraud, for example, are all also included in this total number. Still, the number of evaluations would total several hundred. The Swedish NAB fulfills the dual function of advising how to do evaluations and of carrying them out.

Most other audit offices in Europe, with their traditions of several centuries, may be less prone to adopt the new terminology and therefore appear to have been rather inactive in this field until recently. In practice, however, their work might not be all that different (while the numbers are definitely smaller) from that of the U.S. GAO. Nevertheless, that entire programs are evaluated by European audit offices might be unusual, except for spending on defense equipment programs. However, the concept of policy evaluation seems to have spread to these auditing institutions recently.

Finance ministry initiatives Another source of initiatives can be the finance ministries or equivalent offices such as the OMB in Washington, D.C. Whereas the parliament and the general accounting office can both be regarded as institutions external to government (in the European sense), we now move to actors in the executive branch as potential initiators. Of course, the audit office reports are fed back into the budgetary process; that is, ex post analyses will have an impact on future budget appropriations and even budget proposals of the finance ministry. The relationship between evaluation and budgeting will change, if the finance ministry is in a position to request evaluations from the program administrators in the departments. As has been pointed out before, this is the case in the FRG. The closeness of this link between budgeting and evaluation depends on the frequency and regularity with which studies are requested; if it is a matter of bargaining between finance and program departments, it is likely that evaluations are sacrificed in order to minimize conflict. A structural solution to cope with this problem might be seen in the establishment of an Agency for Policy Analysis with the Dutch Finance Ministry, whereas the Danish system of annually rotating evaluations from policy area to policy area is a procedural device for linking evaluation more firmly to budgeting.

Obviously, the standing of finance departments varies from country to country. It remains to be seen if, in the context of the management initiatives, finance departments will assume as strong positions as the OMB in Washington has enjoyed. Again the question arises whether the studies labeled "evaluations" which finance departments request for legitimizing annual budget proposals deserve this name despite their necessarily quick and short preparation.

Central political initiatives Taking the initiative to institutionalize evaluation procedures in government does not imply that the head of government, or the cabinet, or the cabinet office as the central political actors also initiate specific evaluation studies. Technically this is hardly possible for smaller programs or projects, unless these become a matter of political concern when public criticism arises or principles are at stake and are brought up by a minister. The suggestion to evaluate the respective program will, however, regularly be made by the respective cabinet minister and, therefore, will constitute a departmental initiative. Possibly, a cabinet office would suggest an evaluation owing to its intimate knowledge of departmental affairs.

What central political actors are likely to do is take the initiative to "assess" policies rather than programs; that is, they deal with broader policy or problem areas, which occasionally cut across departmental jurisdictions. They are interested in comprehensive analyses referring to these questions. The broader and the more unspecific the problem under consideration, the more likely is their treatment in commissions and committees. The inverse suggests specific program assessments could be done by in-house specialists. Examples of both, broad approach and central specialist evaluator, can be found in Britain: the former Central Policy Review Staff was an institution directly reporting to the cabinet, and it reviewed broad policy problems and developed new options. The Efficiency Unit followed this line after 1979; its effort to make the machinery of government more efficient involved, however, less substantive studies but rather organizational-reform studies aiming, among other things, at departmental self-evaluation.

Since 1981, the Dutch cabinet decides on the subjects (about one hundred topics through 1988) to be assessed by departmental study groups within the annual Reconsiderations Procedure. The focus of these studies is, however, not confined to questions of program efficiency and effectiveness, but involves organizational aspects, too. The OMB in Washington should also find mention here, as it carries out central budgeting functions and is a central government office. Obviously, the OMB is a central initiator, as it requests evaluations from the departments.

In conclusion, it might be maintained that at the center of government in most countries no initiatives are taken to evaluate specific programs and projects. The exceptions to the rule are the U.S. OMB, whose initiatives derive rather from its budgeting function than from its political staff function; the British Efficiency Unit, which initiates evaluations to the extent they are part of the policy to improve management operations; and the Dutch cabinet, which takes specific evaluation decisions.

Generally one can state that the center of government, apart from emphasizing the need for evaluations and institutionalizing the function, engenders at best broad policy appraisals, which in and of themselves do not meet the formal requirements of a thorough evaluation. These assessments and appraisals, as they are often termed, are then prepared by central government staff units or by advisors and committees.

Departmental initiatives As was mentioned above, departments tend to resist self-evaluation; thus parliaments and their support agencies, as well as cabinets, for this reason have institutionalized or propagated departmental evaluations. Consequently, any of what may appear at a first glance as departmental initiatives are in fact externally induced. Examples are the Swedish central agencies which are responsible to government for evaluating their programs. Nevertheless, there are genuine departmental initiatives. The evaluation efforts in connection with the intervention programs of the 1960s seem to have originated in the respective departments; the more so the greater the affinity between program administrators and relevant outside researchers who dealt with the problem the new program was designed to cope with. In Washington, more than 80 percent of the departmental and agency evaluations in 1984 were internally mandated – in every second case by a top agency official, whereas only 9 percent were requested by Congress and 3 percent by the OMB. This distribution is typical for the rest of the nations and reflects the maturity of the U.S. evaluation tradition as well as the enormous personnel capacities of the evaluation units in Washington.

From a government-wide perspective these decentralized initiatives clustered in certain policy areas (education, employment, health care, developmental aid) and did not involve or cover the majority of departments.

In order to steady the autonomous intradepartmental initiatives or to initiate evaluations in those so-far inactive departments, departmental evaluation units were created. These units range from those which plan and design studies and write reports without necessarily doing the actual research involved, to those which take on all aspects of evaluations. Staff units (206) were observed across all U.S. nondefense departments. In some German ministries (Developmental Aid, Traffic, Press Office, Agriculture, Technology) evaluation units are established. In Denmark these units exist in the departments of Developmental Aid and Labor and the Directorate of Welfare. In Norway the Ministry of Development Cooperation created an evaluation division in 1983.

Making the deputy ministers in Canada responsible for departmental evaluations can be regarded as a functional alternative to the staff solution. In Sweden, expert groups attached to most of the ministries are involved in evaluation activities. In the Netherlands departmental studies are prepared under the Reconsideration Procedure with Finance Ministry officials participating in the work.

To summarize the answers to the question of who initiates evaluation studies in the policy process, one can probably say that in most political systems we meet a multiplicity of stake holders. This fragmentation largely fits the picture we had arrived at in the previous sections with respect to the process of institutionalization. Apart from external institutionalizations and recurrent initiatives, the executive branch itself takes initiatives to evaluate its own activities (to put it carefully). As to the central management units, initiatives can originate in the finance department and become part of routine budgeting. Central political actors, though, tend to restrict themselves to strengthening the inclinations of departments to undertake evaluations at all, while broad policy appraisals of the commission-type can hardly be regarded as evaluations proper. On the decentralized level of the departments, evaluation activities are increasingly preprogrammed by legislated evaluation requests. Furthermore, the evaluation function, partly in response, tends to be structurally differentiated from the function of the program manager.

Internal versus External Evaluation Research

Initiatives for evaluation are usually directed at actors other than the initiator himself, nor do those responsible for presenting evaluation results always carry out the necessary research for preparing the report. When we ask who actually evaluates a program, we find that evaluation research is only partly done within the structural units mentioned above. Rare cases of in-house research are complemented by an overwhelming amount of commissioned external research.

In-house research To carry out evaluation studies within the politico-administrative system requires at least specific jobs and at best professional policy analysts familiar with evaluation methodology. In the U.S. executive branch (1984), 1,179 professional staff members were occupied in evaluation units and consequently only one-quarter of the 1,689 studies in 1984 were conducted externally. In addition, at any point in time, the GAO is conducting another several hundred in-house PE studies.

The extent to which in-house research is carried out in government departments might strongly depend on a government's organizational principles. In most countries the ruling principle is that departments should be as small as possible and serve the minister as his staff; under these circumstances the ministry would be badly advised to engage in research activities. What the ministry will do, however, is to formulate the policy conclusions drawn from a research report, whereas the research activity would either be delegated to governmental and quasi-autonomous governmental or nongovernmental research agencies, or commissioned to outside researchers. Federal government research agencies, for instance in the FRG, are numerous in technical policy areas (agriculture, traffic, commerce).

Of course, the picture is different where the task of the organization, say the GAO, is to evaluate departmental programs. Here the research activity is the core of the agency's mission.

External research As a rule the executive branch, thus, will transfer evaluations, which involve research activities, to specialists outside the administration. These can be either government-controlled institutions or independent centers, such as academic or commercial contractors (see Wagner and Wollmann 1986b).

Examples of government-controlled research agencies in the FRG include the Research Institute of the Labor Market Administration (founded in 1969), the Science Center of Berlin (1973), or most of the nationally important economic research institutes like the Deutsches Institut für Wirtschaftsforschung in Berlin. Sweden has a number of sectoral policy research institutes which, although being part of government, have a high degree of academic freedom. In this respect the statistical offices will also be potential research institutes to deal with evaluations. Government control or sponsorship does not imply that the research is scientifically dependent and possibly biased, but rather that government is in a position to ask the institute to investigate a certain question.

The availability of independent institutions reflects the applied character of a national social-science culture. While some countries give research predominantly to universities (particularly in education policy), others may be in a position to draw on independent institutions like the Brookings Institution in Washington, D.C., U.S.A., or on semiautonomous institutions like the Danish National Institute of Social Research (founded in 1958) or Denmark's Local Government's Research Institute on Public Finance and Administration (founded in 1975); furthermore, in the 1970s Canada founded the C. D. Howe Institute and the Institute for Research on Public Policy.

Where surveys (sampling, interviewing) are necessary to analyze a program, it is more likely that commercial research institutes become involved. These institutes can be found in most of the countries under consideration, although their number naturally varies according to the size of the research market.

Administration of External Research

If evaluations are externally contracted, the interaction between researcher and administrator becomes problematic and is often dealt with in the literature analyzing the process of giving policy advice; I shall not embark on this problem but only deal with three aspects here.

Contracting evaluation researchers Has evaluation research become competitive? In principle, it is favorable for the mandating government official if he can choose between alternative external researchers; from a purely economical point of view, government will wish to contract the qualitatively best and least expensive evaluator. Political considerations may play a role, too, and induce the government to give a contract to an institute whose views are similar to those of the program administrator.

In practice, however, in most countries the supply side might be not so strongly developed that there are alternatives to choose from. It is indicative of the state of the art that the U.S. data show three-quarters of the four hundred research contracts (1984) following competition between contractors. In particular, in smaller countries one cannot expect an evaluation market big enough for equally specialized institutes to develop. In Sweden, therefore, most of the studies under responsibility of ministerial research delegations are commissioned to universities or public-sectoral research institutes.

If quality control of research is a problem in general, it is all the more the concern with sole-source contracts. One of the few quality-control mechanisms available for sole-source contracts is to make sure that the final results are published and thus open to public scrutiny and study by other researchers.

Financing evaluations The costs of evaluations are high and not seldom cost up to a million or more of the national currency; in particular in the United States evaluation has become a multimillion-dollar business (with 20 percent of the 1,775 evaluations in the United States in 1984 costing more than one hundred thousand dollars). Unfortunately, we do not have data from other countries. Often, the budget is not clear enough to allow inferences in this respect, or evaluation resources are hidden behind various items. At best the volume of government research could be determined irrespective of type.

The source of evaluation funds varies with the arrangements and structure of the evaluation system. With evaluation offices and in-house research the costs are basically covered by the institution's budget. If research takes place external to the bureaucracy, the source of funds can be with the mandator of the evaluation, for example, parliament, or with the program administration. Furthermore, the funds can be dispersed over many budget items or centralized in a departmental, government-wide or parliamentary research budget. The more firmly evaluation is institutionalized, the more likely it is that there will be the allocation of specific funds, for example, to a departmental evaluation unit. An interesting variation of this arrangement has been devised in the United States, where evaluation funds are occasionally earmarked and stipulated within the legislation creating the program itself.

Dissemination of studies A central political aspect of the evaluation process is the extent to which the studies are circulated. Obviously, reports to parliament are important and can provide the stimulus for a broad political discussion about the future of a program. For this very reason, evaluations undertaken or contracted by government departments tend to be secluded from the public. The practice depends on legal norms regulating the freedom of information. Naturally, the degree of secrecy or publicity attached to this kind of information is determined by the national political and administrative cultures. It can be taken for granted that freedom in this respect is largest in the United States, Scandinavia, and the Netherlands, whereas Britain might keep reports, unless addressed to Parliament, even more secret than the FRG. In Germany researchers are considering whether to accept government contracts only if subsequent publication of research reports is safeguarded. Practically, however, the question of public access to research reports has never been a problem: it is impossible to keep secrets in Bonn.

Publication involves more than public access; reports would have to be printed. The costs of publication, though, has nowhere been a problem.

Concluding Remarks

In writing this summary I became increasingly aware of the fact that the availability of data on the national evaluation arrangements is itself an indicator of the state of the art in the various countries. The more firmly evaluation is institutionalized and the longer its tradition, the greater the propensity to analyze and even evaluate the evaluation business and to engage in meta-evaluation research. Therefore, the tentativeness of this summary reflects the still-shaky state of evaluation in many of the countries considered here.

This weakness pertains also to the very concept of evaluation. Where the evaluation function is firmly institutionalized and a tradition of evaluation research has developed, the term is employed in the narrow sense of methodologically controlled analysis of program strategies and impacts. In other countries, it has a rather broad connotation embracing various feedback mechanisms apart from research-based ones and a multiplicity of criteria beyond that of effectiveness.

I would not go so far as to maintain that the second wave of evaluations, which was primarily initiated by parliaments and the political executive putting the auditing institutions into the limelight, tended to water down the concept of evaluation. There are, however, strong indications that the further the evaluation function moves away from the departmental program manager, the more it becomes amalgamated with traditional auditing and review practices focusing also on input, output, and legality of implementation and not merely on strategy and impact of programs.

Note

1. The name of the BOB was changed to Office of Management and Budget (OMB) in 1970, as PPBS was intermittently called Planning Programming Evaluation System (Schick 1971).

References

Adams, B., and B. Sherman. 1978. "Sunset implementation: A positive partnership to make government work." *Public Administration Review* 38, 78–81.

Bulmer, M. 1988. "Social science expertise and executive-bureaucratic politics in Britain. *Governance* 1, 26–49.

Nioche, J.-P., and R. Poinsard. 1985. "Public policy evaluation in France." *Journal of Policy Analysis and Management* 5, 58–72.

Quermonne, J.-L., and L. Rouban. 1986. "French public administration and policy evaluation: The quest for accountability." *Public Administration Review* 46, 397–406.

Rossi, P. H., and S. R. Wright. 1977. "Evaluation research: An assessment of theory, practice, and politics." *Evaluation Quarterly* 1, 5–52.

Schick, A. 1971. "From analysis to evaluation." *The Annals of the American Academy of Political and Social Science* pp. 57–71.

———. 1988. "Micro-budgetary adaptations to fiscal stress in industrialized democracies." *Public Administration Review* 48, 523–33.

Wagner, P., and H. Wollmann. 1986a. "Fluctuations in the development of evaluation research: Do "regime shifts" matter?" *International Social Science Journal* 205–18.

———. 1986b. "Social scientists in policy research and consulting: Some cross-national comparisons." *International Social Science Journal* 601–17.

Ysander, B.-C. 1983. "Public policy evaluation in Sweden." The Industrial Institute for Economic and Social Research. Working paper no. 106.

Index

About the Editor

Ray C. Rist is Director of Operations for the General Government Division, United States General Accounting Office. Dr. Rist joined GAO in 1981. His extensive knowledge of evaluation design principles has helped construct the proper analytical framework for GAO jobs as diverse as reviews of defense programs to education and employment strategies. His work in the area of program evaluation and policy analysis spans nearly twenty years, involving him in countless studies at the local, state, national, and international levels.

Dr. Rist contributed to various academic and professional efforts prior to his joining GAO. From 1977 to 1981, he was national director of the Youthwork National Policy Study on youth employment and training programs and professor at Cornell University. Also, Dr. Rist worked from 1974 to 1976 with the National Institute of Education (NIE) in several capacities on planning and implementing research and evaluation programs in the areas of school desegregation, bilingual education, school violence, and services for disadvantaged students. He left NIE in 1976 to accept an appointment as Senior Fulbright Fellow at the Max Planck Institute in Berlin, West Germany. While there, he evaluated various social, educational, and economic policies regarding the "guestworker" population in Germany. From 1968 to 1974, he was a sociology professor, first in Illinois and then in Oregon.

Dr. Rist earned his Ph.D. in sociology and anthropology in 1970 from Washington University (St. Louis). His list of book and article publications is extensive. His 15 books have been published by, among others, Harvard University Press, M.I.T. Press, Transaction Publishers, Columbia University Press, and Klett-Cotta Press of Stuttgart, Germany. His most recent books are *Policy Issues for the 1990s*, (Transaction Publishers, 1989) and *Finding Work: Cross-National Perspectives on Employment and Training Policy* (Falmer Press, 1987). He has lectured in more than twenty countries and served as a consultant to many international organizations.

Addresses of Authors

Albaek, Erik
Institute of Political Science
University of Aarhus
Universitetsparken
DK-8000 Aarhus C
Denmark

Bemelmans-Videc, Marie Louise
Department of Public
    Administration
State University of Leiden
Rapenburg 59
3211 GJ Leiden
Netherlands

Derlien, Hans-Ulrich
Feldkirchenstrasse 21
University of Bamberg
8600 Bamberg
Federal Republic of Germany

Elte, Ronald
Department of Public
    Administration
State University of Leiden
Rapenburg 59
3211 GJ Leiden
Netherlands

Eriksen, Bjarne
Directorate of Organization and
    Management
Box 8115 Dep.
Oslo 1
Norway

Gray, Andrew
Eliot College
University of Kent
Canterbury
Kent CT2 7NY
England

Jenkins, Bill
Darwin College
University of Kent
Canterbury
Kent CT2 7NY
England

Koolhaas, E.
Department of Public
    Administration
State University of Leiden
Rapenburg 59
3211 GJ Leiden
Netherlands

Horber-Papazian, Katia
Community of Study for Regional
    Development
Federal Polytechnic
14 Avenue de l'Eglise Anglaise
Ch-1001 Lausanne
Switzerland

Rist, Ray C.
General Government Division
United States General Accounting
    Office
441 G Street, NW
Washington, DC
20548 USA

Segsworth, Robert V.
Diploma Program in Public
    Administration
Laurentian University
Sudbury, Ontario P3E 2C6
Canada

Thévoz, Laurent
Community of Study for Regional
    Development
Federal Polytechnic
14 Avenue de l'Eglise Anglaise
Ch-1001 Lausanne
Switzerland

Winter, Søren
Institute of Political Science
University of Aarhus
Universitetsparken
DK-8000 Aarhus C.
Denmark